ESTATE PUBL...

G000135598

WILTSHIRE

Street maps with index
Administrative Districts
Population Gazetteer
Road Map with index
Postcodes

COUNTY RED BOOKS

This atlas is intended for those requiring street maps of the historical and commercial centres of towns within the county. Each locality is normally presented on one or two pages and although, with many small towns, this space is sufficient to portray the whole urban area, the maps of large towns and cities are for centres only and are not intended to be comprehensive. Such coverage in Super and Local Red Books (see page 2).

Every effort has been made to verify the accuracy of information in this book but the publishers cannot accept responsibility for expense or loss caused by any error or omission. Information that will be of assistance to the user of these maps will be welcomed.

The representation of a road, track or footpath on the maps in this atlas is no evidence of the existence of a right of way.

Street plans prepared and published by ESTATE PUBLICATIONS, Bridewell House, TENTERDEN, KENT, and based upon the ORDNANCE SURVEY mapping with the permission of the Controller of H. M. Stationery Office.

The Publishers acknowledge the co-operation of the local authorities of towns represented in this atlas.

Estate Publications 184 H   ISBN 1 84192 045 2   © Crown Copyright 398713

COUNTY RED BOOK

WILTSHIRE

contains street maps for each town centre

SUPER & LOCAL RED BOOKS

are street atlases with comprehensive local coverage

SALISBURY & WILTON

including: Amesbury, Downton, Mere,
Redlynch, Tisbury etc.

SWINDON

including: Calne, Chippenham,
Marlborough etc.

CONTENTS

COUNTY ADMINISTRATIVE DISTRICTS: pages 4-5

GAZETTEER INDEX TO ROAD MAP: pages 6-7
(with populations)

COUNTY ROAD MAP: pages 8-11

TOWN CENTRE STREET MAPS:

LEGEND TO STREET MAPS

One-Way Street	→	Post Office	●
Pedestrianized	▨	Public Convenience	C
Car Park	P	Place of Worship	+

Scale of street plans: 4 Inches to 1 mile (unless otherwise stated on the map).

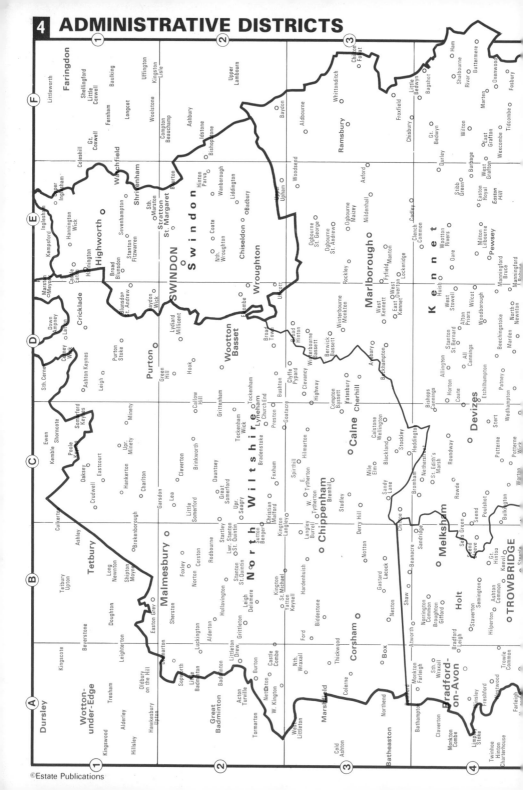

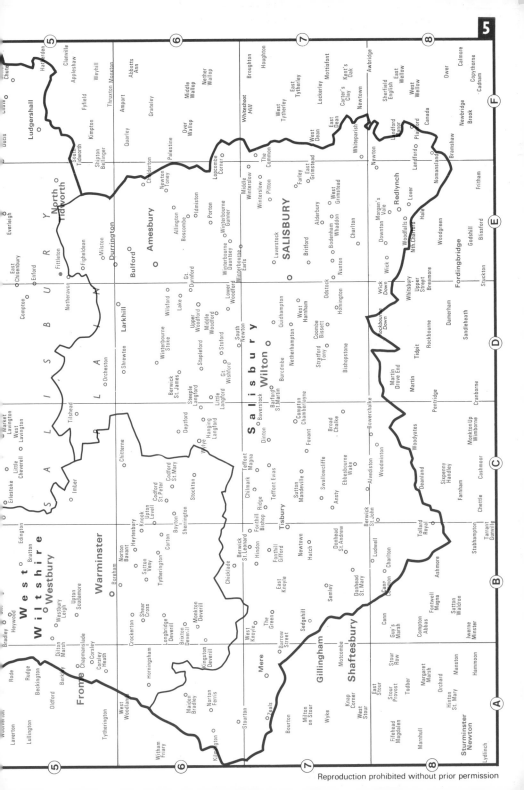

Reproduction prohibited without prior permission

GAZETTEER INDEX TO ROAD MAP
with Populations
County of Wiltshire population **564,471**

Wiltshire Districts:

Kennett	68,526
North Wiltshire	111,974
Salisbury	105,318
Thamesdown	170,850
West Wiltshire	107,803

Aldbourne **1,682**		9 G3
Alderbury **1,859**		11 F9
Alderton		8 B2
All Cannings **555**		9 E5
Allington **469**		8 D5
Allington		11 F8
Alton Priors **230**		9 E5
Alvediston **85**		10 C10
Amesbury **6,656**		11 F7
Ansty **100**		10 C9
Ashton Common		8 B5
Ashton Keynes **1,399**		8 D1
Atworth **943**		8 B4
Avebury **562**		9 E4
Axford		9 F4
Badbury		9 F3
Bagshot		9 G4
Barford St Martin **568**		10 D9
Barrow Street		10 B9
Baverstock		10 D8
Baydon **512**		9 G3
Beanacre		8 C4
Beckhampton		9 E4
Beechingstoke **147**		9 E5
Berwick Bassett **51**		9 E4
Berwick St James **153**		10 D8
Berwick St John **260**		10 C10
Berwick St Leonard **34**		10 C8
Biddestone **466**		8 B3
Bishops Cannings **1032**		8 D5
Bishopstone (Salisbury) **566**		10 D9
Bishopstone (Swindon) **620**		9 G2
Bishopstrow **112**		*
Blackland		8 D4
Blunsdon St Andrew **2,195**		9 E1
Bodenham		11 F9
Boreham		10 C7
Boscombe		11 F8
Bowerchalke **335**		10 D10
Box **3,789**		8 B4
Boyton **162**		10 C8
Bradenstoke		8 D3
Bradford Leigh		8 B5
Bradford-on-Avon **8,815**		8 B5
Bratton **1,193**		10 C6
Braydon **49**		*
Bremhill **984**		8 C4
Brinkworth **1,167**		8 D2
Britford **440**		11 F9
Brixton Deverill **63**		10 B8
Broad Blunsden		9 E1
Broad Chalke **584**		10 D9
Broad Hinton **629**		9 E3
Broad Town **567**		9 E3
Brokenborough **199**		8 C2
Bromham **1,860**		8 C4
Broughton Gifford **901**		8 B5
Bulford **5,255**		11 F7
Bulkington **268**		8 C5
Burbage **1,434**		9 F5
Burcombe **151**		10 D9
Burton		8 B3
Bushton		8 D3
Buttermere **43**		9 H5
Cadley		9 F4
Callow Hill		8 D2
Calne **13,530**		8 D4

Calstone Wellington		8 D4
Castle Combe **347**		8 B3
Castle Eaton **225**		9 E1
Chapmanslade **588**		10 B7
Charlton (Malmesbury) **428**		8 C2
Charlton (Salisbury)		11 F9
Charlton (Shaftesbury)		10 C10
Charlton (Upavon) **77**		11 E6
Cherhill **712**		8 D4
Cheverell Magna **539**		10 C6
Cheverell Parva **176**		10 D6
Chicklade **71**		10 C8
Chilmark **425**		10 C8
Chilton Foliat **299**		9 G4
Chippenham **25,794**		8 C3
Chirton **409**		10 E6
Chisbury		9 G4
Chiseldon **2,651**		9 F3
Chitterne **289**		10 D7
Chittoe		8 C4
Cholderton **200**		11 F7
Christian Malford **681**		8 C3
Church End		8 D3
Chute (Upr. & Lwr.) **309**		11 G6
Chute Forest **146**		*
Clarendon Park **269**		*
Clench Common		9 F4
Clevancy		8 D3
Cleverton (with Lea) **766**		8 D2
Cliffe Pypard **323**		9 E3
Coate (Devizes)		8 D5
Coate (Swindon)		9 F2
Codford St Mary		10 C8
Codford St Peter		10 C7
Colerne **2,572**		8 B4
Collingbourne Ducis **802**		11 G6
Collingbourne Kingston **454**		11 F6
Compton		11 E6
Compton Bassett **271**		8 D4
Compton Chamberlayne **85**		10 D9
Coombe Bissett **653**		11 E9
Corsham **10,549**		8 B4
Corsley **731**		10 B7
Corsley Heath		10 B7
Corston		8 C2
Corton		10 C7
Covingham **4,128**		*
Cricklade **4,099**		9 E1
Crockerton		10 B7
Crudwell **948**		8 C1
Dauntsey **471**		8 D2
Deptford		10 D8
Derry Hill		8 C4
Devizes **11,250**		8 D5
Dilton Marsh **1,924**		10 B6
Dinton **536**		10 D9
Donhead St Andrew **422**		10 C9
Donhead St Mary **981**		10 C9
Downton **2,784**		11 F10
Durley		9 F5
Durrington **6,926**		11 F7
East Chisenbury		11 E6
Eastcott		10 D6
East Coulston **151**		10 C6
Eastcourt		8 D1
Easterton **591**		10 D6
East Grafton (with West) **603**		9 G5
East Grimstead (with West) **514**		11 F9
East Kennett **100**		9 E4
East Knoyle **645**		10 B9
Easton Grey **70**		8 B2
Easton Royal **260**		9 F5
East Tytherton		8 C3
Ebbesbourne Wake **198**		10 D9

Edington **716**		10 C6
Elcombe		9 E3
Enford **655**		11 E6
Erlestoke **285**		10 C6
Etchilhampton **162**		8 D5
Everleigh **249**		11 F6
Farley (with Pitton) **704**		11 F9
Figheldean **675**		11 E7
Firsdown **611**		*
Fittleton **370**		11 E6
Fonthill Bishop **112**		10 C8
Fonthill Gifford **108**		10 C9
Ford		8 B3
Fosbury		9 G5
Fovant **641**		10 D9
Foxham		8 D3
Foxley		8 C2
Froxfield **356**		9 G4
Fyfield **191**		9 E4
Garsdon		8 C2
Gastard		8 B4
Goatacre		8 D3
Great Bedwyn **1,093**		9 G5
Great Durnford **405**		11 E8
Great Hinton **212**		8 C5
Great Somerford **734**		8 C2
Great Wishford **360**		11 E8
Green Hill		8 D2
Grittenham		8 D2
Grittleton **373**		8 B3
Ham **175**		9 H5
Hanging Langford		10 D8
Hankerton **314**		8 C1
Hannington **228**		9 F1
Hannington Wick		9 F1
Hardenhuish		8 C3
Hatch		10 C9
Hawkeridge		10 B6
Haydon Wick **7,417**		9 E2
Heddington **364**		8 D4
Heytesbury **643**		10 C7
Heywood **459**		10 B6
Highway		8 D3
Highworth **8,668**		9 F1
Hilmarton **798**		8 D3
Hilperton **2,632**		8 B5
Hindon **493**		10 C8
Hinton Parva		9 F2
Holt **1,458**		8 B5
Homington		11 E9
Hook		9 E2
Horningsham **418**		10 B7
Horton		8 D5
Huish **54**		9 E5
Hullavington **1,122**		8 B2
Idmiston **2,177**		11 F8
Imber		10 C7
Inglesham **117**		9 F1
Keevil **404**		8 C5
Kilmington **282**		10 A8
Kingston Deverill **267**		10 B8
Kington Langley **718**		8 C3
Kington St Michael **695**		8 C3
Knook **61**		10 C7
Lacock **1,068**		8 C4
Lake		11 E8
Landford **1,195**		11 G10
Landford Manor		11 G10
Langley Burrell **412**		8 C3
Larkhill		11 E7
Latton **372**		9 E1
Laverstock **3,029**		11 F9

6

Place	Pop.	Grid
Lea (with Cleverton)	**766**	8 C2
Leigh	**283**	8 D1
Leigh Delamere		8 B3
Liddington	**343**	9 F2
Limpley Stoke	**627**	9 A5
Little Bedwyn	**286**	9 G4
Little Langford		10 D8
Little Somerford	**416**	8 C2
Littleton Drew		8 B3
Littleton Pannell		10 D6
Lockeridge		9 E4
Longbridge Deverill	**851**	10 B7
Lopcombe Corner		11 F8
Lover		11 F10
Lower Stanton St Quintin		8 C3
Lower Woodford		11 E8
Luckington	**508**	8 B2
Ludgershall	**3,379**	11 G6
Ludwell		10 C10
Lydiard Millicent	**1,203**	9 E2
Lydiard Tregoze	**382**	*
Lyneham	**4,747**	8 D3
Maiden Bradley	**328**	10 A8
Malmesbury	**3,999**	8 C2
Manningford Bohune		9 E5
Manningford Bruce		9 E5
Manton		9 F4
Marden	**155**	9 E5
Market Lavington	**1,858**	10 D6
Marlborough	**6,788**	9 E4
Marston	**142**	8 C5
Marston Meysey	**209**	9 E1
Marten		9 G5
Melksham	**12,788**	8 C5
Mere	**2,257**	10 B8
Middle Winterslow		11 F8
Middle Woodford		11 E8
Mildenhall	**472**	9 F4
Mile Elm		8 D4
Milston	**126**	11 F7
Milton Lilbourne	**484**	9 F5
Minety	**1,325**	8 D1
Monkton Deverill		10 B8
Monkton Farleigh	**478**	8 B4
Morgan's Vale		11 F10
Neston		8 B4
Netheravon	**1,146**	11 E6
Netherhampton	**158**	11 E9
Netherstreet		8 D4
Nettleton	**569**	8 B3
Newton Toney	**373**	11 F8
Newtown		10 C9
Normansland		11 F10
Norrington Common		8 B5
North Bradley	**1,770**	10 B6
North Newnton	**414**	9 E5
North Tidworth	**5,813**	11 F6
North Wraxall	**360**	8 B3
North Wroughton		9 F2
Norton	**114**	8 B2
Norton Bavant	**109**	10 C7
Norton Ferris		10 A8
Notton		8 C4
Nunton		11 E9
Oaksey	**443**	8 D1
Oare		9 F5
Odstock	**548**	11 E9
Ogbourne Maizey		9 F4
Ogbourne St Andrew	**262**	9 F4
Ogbourne St George	**399**	9 F3
Orcheston	**282**	10 D7
Oxenwood		9 G5
Patney	**149**	8 D5
Pewsey	**2,831**	9 F5
Pitton (with Farley)	**704**	11 F9
Plaitford		11 G10
Porton		11 F8
Potterne	**1,590**	8 D5
Potterne Wick		8 D5
Poulshot	**352**	8 C5
Preshute	**160**	*
Preston		8 D3
Purton	**3,879**	9 E2
Purton Stoke		9 E1
Quidhampton	**363**	11 E9
Ramsbury	**1,877**	9 G4
Redlynch	**3,158**	11 F10
Ridge		10 C8
Rivar		9 G5
Rockley		9 E4
Rodbourne		8 C2
Roundway	**1,633**	8 D5
Rowde	**1,294**	8 C5
Rushall	**114**	10 E6
St Edith's Marsh		8 D5
Salisbury	**36,890**	11 F9
Sandridge		8 C4
Sandy Lane		8 C4
Savernake	**194**	*
Sedgehill & Semley	**584**	10 B9
Seend	**1,089**	8 C5
Seend Cleeve		8 C5
Sells Green		8 C5
Semington	**803**	8 C5
Sevenhampton		9 F1
Shalbourne	**550**	9 G5
Shaw		8 B4
Sherrington	**70**	10 C8
Shear Cross		10 B7
Sherston	**1,372**	8 B2
Shrewton	**1,780**	10 D7
Sopworth	**81**	8 B2
South Marston	**703**	9 F2
South Newton	**696**	11 E8
Southwick	**1,971**	10 B6
South Wraxall	**397**	8 B5
Spirthill		8 D3
Stanton Fitzwarren	**211**	9 F1
Stanton St Bernard	**141**	9 E5
Stanton St Quintin	**747**	8 C3
Stapleford	**249**	11 E8
Startley		8 C2
Staverton	**306**	8 B5
Steeple Ashton	**955**	8 C5
Steeple Langford	**517**	10 D8
Stert	**167**	8 D5
Stibb Green		9 F5
Stockley		8 D4
Stockton	**192**	10 C8
Stoford		11 E8
Stourton	**201**	10 A8
Stratford Toney	**70**	11 E9
Stratton St Margaret	**13,383**	9 F2
Studley		8 C4
Sutton Benger	**904**	8 C3
Sutton Mandeville	**215**	10 D9
Sutton Veny	**585**	10 C7
Swallowcliffe	**184**	10 C9
Swindon	**127,348**	9 E2
Teffont Evias		10 D9
Teffont Magna	**216**	10 D8
The Common		11 F8
The Green		10 B9
Thickwood		8 B4
Tidcombe (with Fosbury)	**105**	9 G5
Tilshead	**343**	10 D7
Tisbury	**1,836**	10 C9
Tockenham	**221**	8 D3
Tockenham Wick		8 D3
Tollard Royal	**106**	10 C10
Trowbridge	**25,279**	8 B5
Trowle Common		8 B5
Tytherington		10 C7
Uffcott		9 E3
Upavon	**1,241**	11 E6
Upper Inglesham		9 F1
Upper Minety		8 D1
Upper Seagry	**270**	8 C3
Upper Upham		9 F3
Upper Woodford	**447**	11 E8
Upton Lovell	**144**	10 C7
Upton Scudamore	**250**	10 B7
Urchfont	**977**	8 D5
Wanborough	**1,478**	9 F2
Warminster	**16,267**	10 B7
Wedhampton		8 D5
West Ashton	**387**	10 B6
Westbury	**9,939**	10 B6
Westbury Leigh		10 B6
West Dean	**220**	11 G9
West Grafton (with East)	**603**	9 F5
West Grimstead (with East) **514**		11 F9
West Harnham		11 E9
West Kennett		9 E4
West Kington		8 B3
West Knoyle	**139**	10 B8
West Lavington	**1,076**	10 D6
West Overton	**629**	9 E4
West Stowell		9 E5
West Tisbury	**577**	*
West Tytherton		8 C3
Westwood	**1,195**	8 B5
Wexcombe		9 G5
Whaddon		11 F9
Whiteparish	**1,313**	11 F10
Whittonditch		9 G4
Wick		11 F10
Wilcot	**549**	9 E5
Wilsford (Amesbury)	**120**	11 E8
Wilsford (Upavon)	**82**	10 E6
Wilton (Marlborough)		9 G5
Wilton (Salisbury)	**3,717**	11 E9
Wingfield	**385**	10 B6
Winsley	**1,834**	8 B5
Winterbourne Bassett	**123**	9 E3
Winterbourne Dauntsey		11 F8
Winterbourne Earls	**1,266**	11 F8
Winterbourne Gunner		11 F8
Winterbourne Monkton	**161**	9 E4
Winterbourne Stoke	**193**	11 E7
Winterslow	**1,836**	11 F8
Woodborough	**264**	9 E5
Woodfalls		11 F10
Woodminton		10 D10
Woodsend		9 F3
Wootton Bassett	**10,524**	9 E2
Wootton Rivers	**271**	9 F5
Worton	**601**	8 C5
Wroughton.	**7,111**	9 E3
Wylye	**409**	10 D8
Yatesbury		8 D4
Yatton Keynell	**656**	8 B3
Zeals	**636**	10 A9

Population figures are based upon the 1991 census and relate to the local authority or parish as constituted at that date. Places with no popoulation figure form part of a larger local authority area or parish. Boundaries of local authority areas are shown on page 4.

Thamesdown Borough Council has now become a Unitary Authority.

Population figures in bold type.

*Places not included on map due to limitation of space.

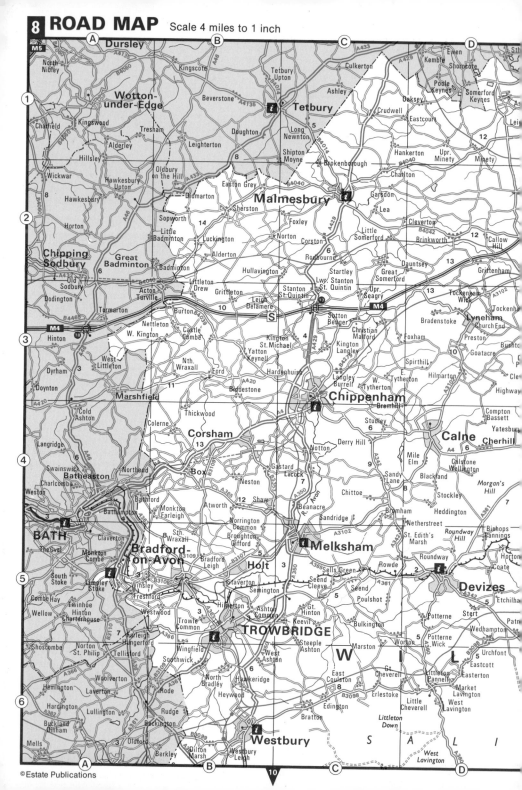

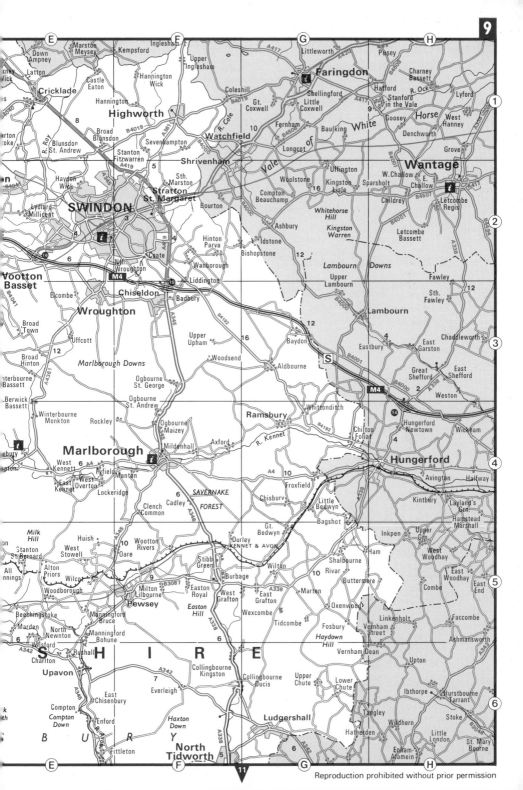

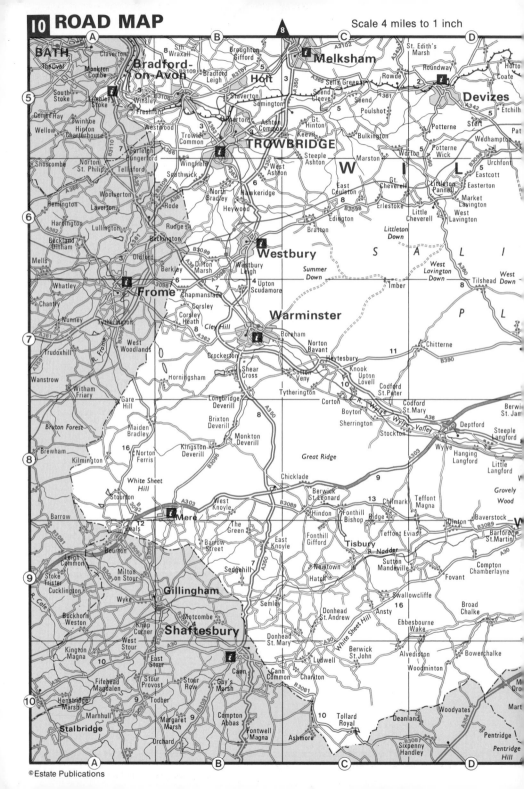

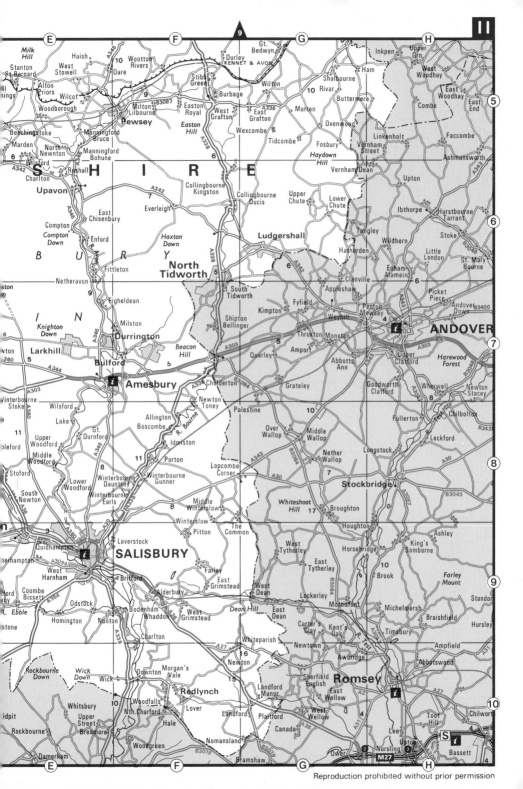

Reproduction prohibited without prior permission

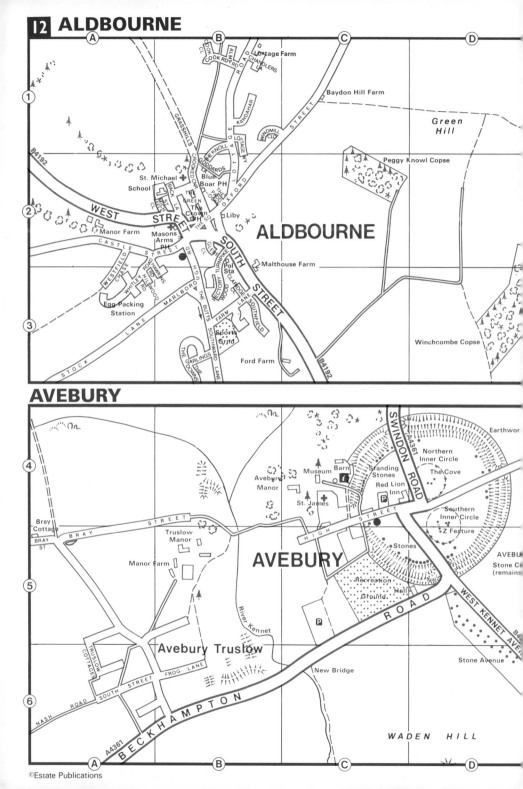

AMESBURY 13

Reproduction prohibited without prior permission

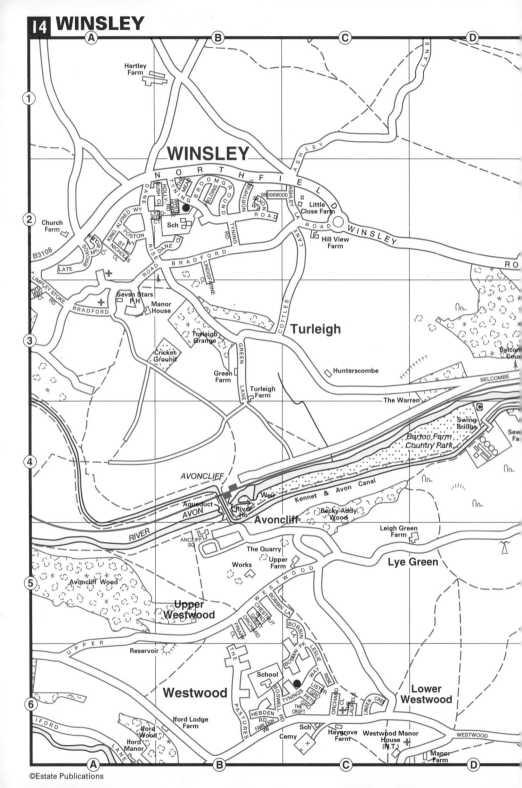

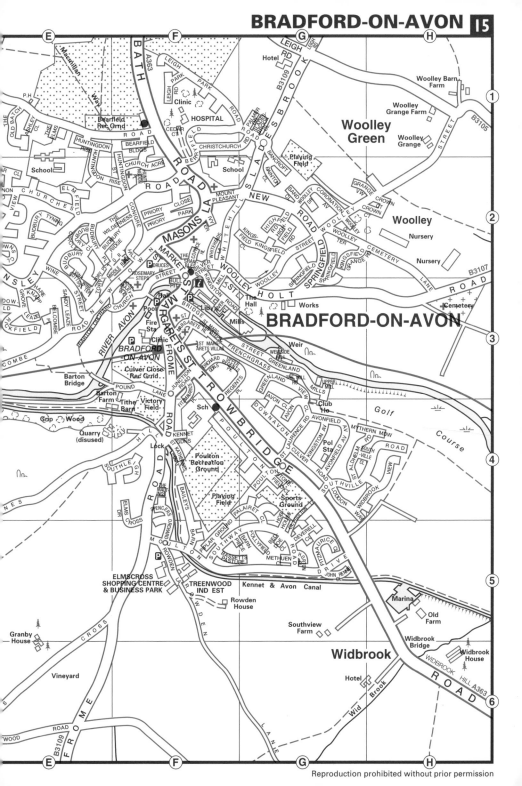

BRADFORD-ON-AVON

Woolley Green

Woolley

Widbrook

Reproduction prohibited without prior permission

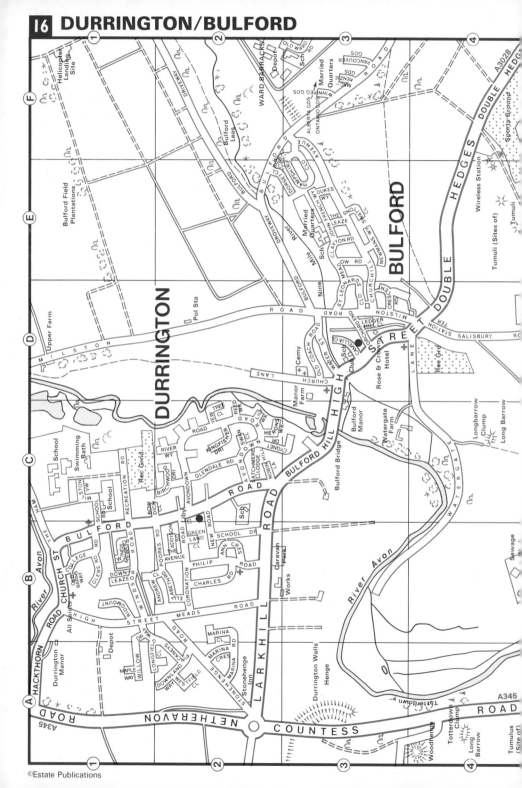

DURRINGTON

BULFORD

©Estate Publications

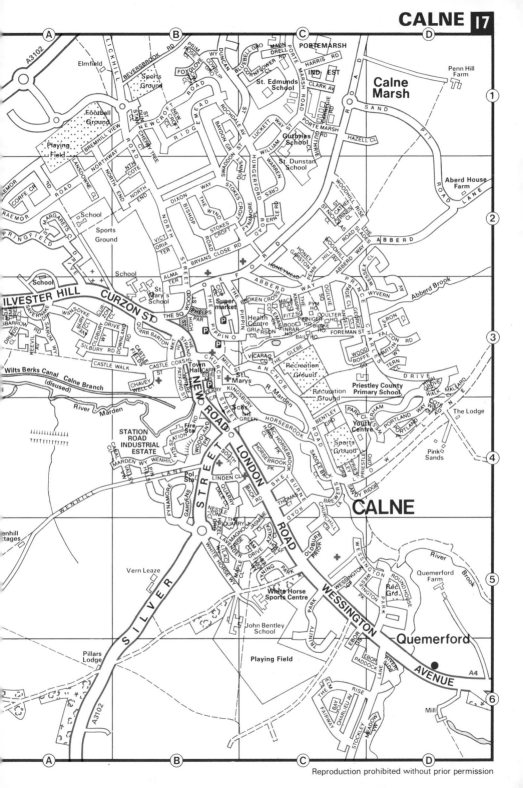

Reproduction prohibited without prior permission

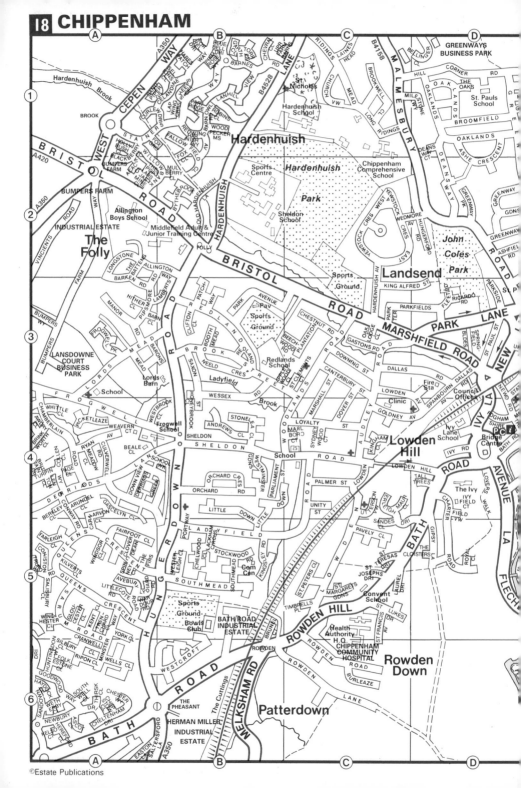

©Estate Publications

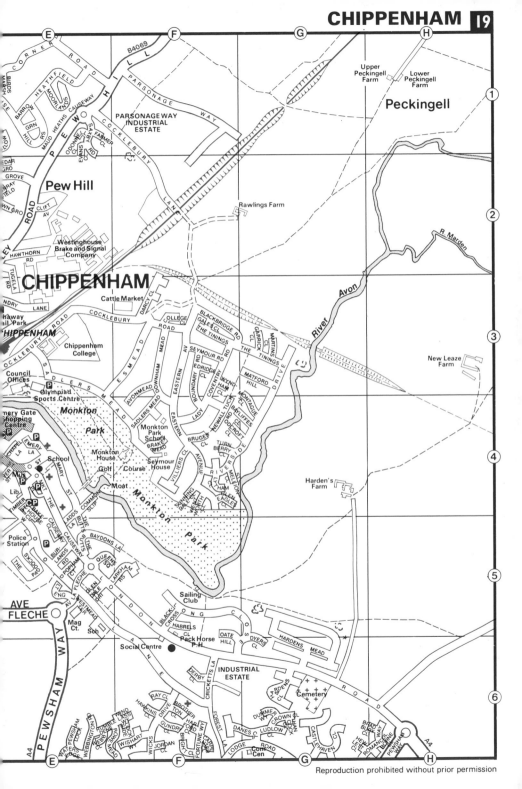

Reproduction prohibited without prior permission

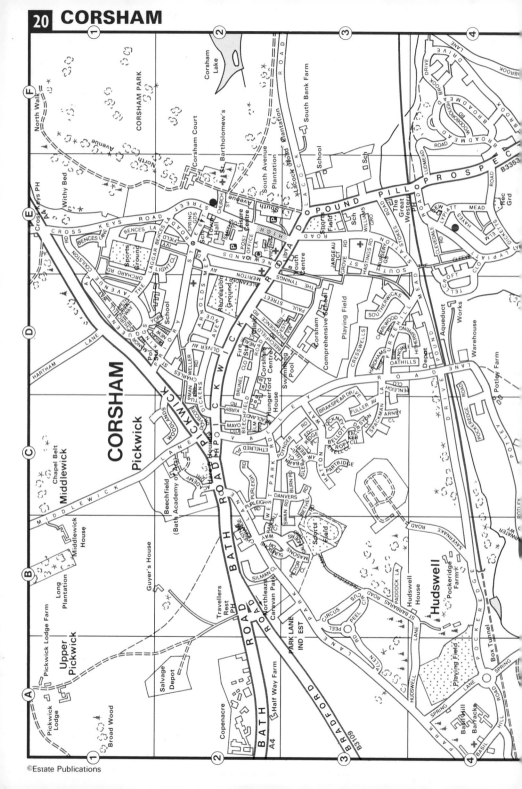

©Estate Publications

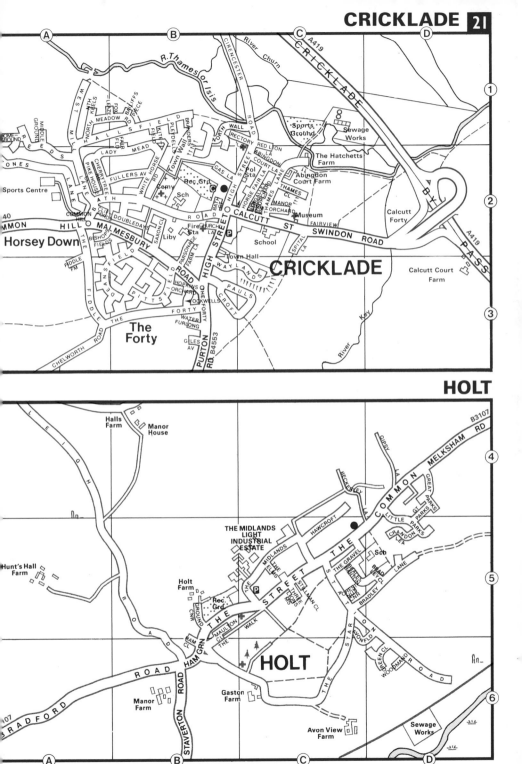

HOLT

Reproduction prohibited without prior permission

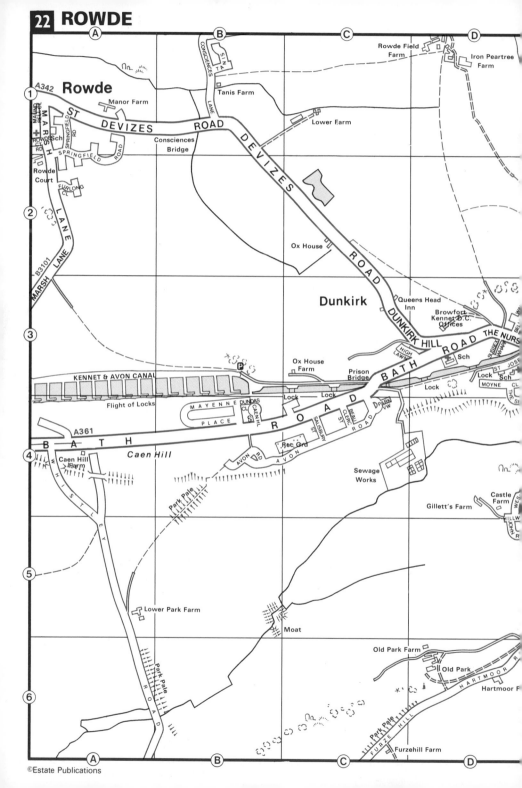

Rowde

Manor Farm

A342

ST DEVIZES ROAD

MARSH LANE

Springfield RD

SPRINGFIELD ROAD

ROWDE RD

Sch

Rowde Court

FURLONG CL

MARSH LANE

B3101

CONSCIENCES LANE

Tanis Farm

STANTA

Consciences Bridge

DEVIZES ROAD

Lower Farm

Rowde Field Farm

Iron Peartree Farm

Ox House

Dunkirk

Queens Head Inn

Browfort

Kennet D.C. Offices

DUNKIRK HILL ROAD

THE NURS

Sch

BATH ROAD

KENNET & AVON CANAL

P

Ox House Farm

HIGH LAWN

Prison Bridge

Sch

St JOS

Lock

Lock

MOYNE CL

St

Flight of Locks

MAYENNE PLACE

DUNDAS CL

CAEN HL GS

Lock

ROAD

PARK VW

D

SALISBURY ST

BEAU CLERC ROAD

A361

BATH

Caen Hill

WHISTLEY

Caen Hill Farm

Park Pale

AVON RD

AVON

Rec Grd

Sewage Works

Gillett's Farm

Castle Farm

HILLW

Lower Park Farm

Park Pale ROAD

Moat

Old Park Farm

Old Park

HARTMOOR R

Hartmoor F

Park Pale

FURZE HILL

Furzehill Farm

1 2 3 4 5 6

A B C D

©Estate Publications

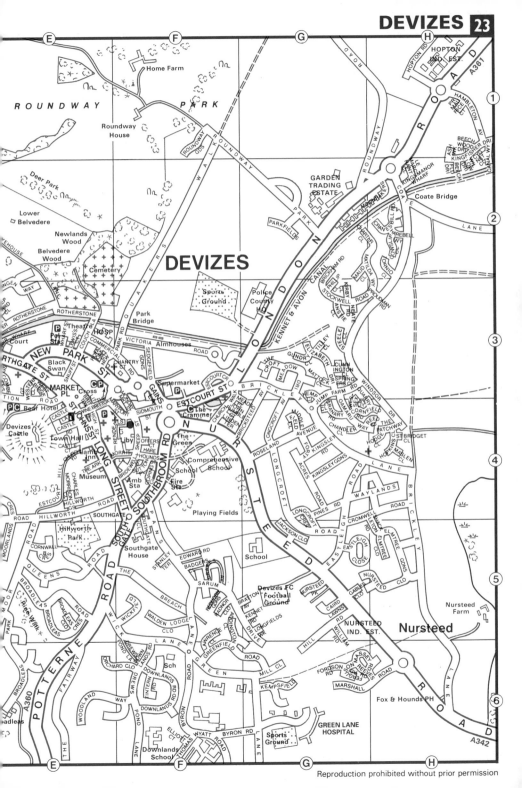

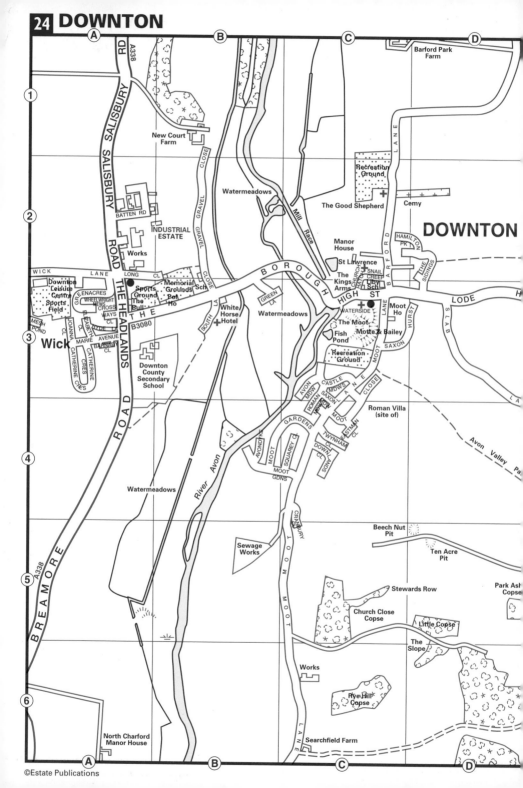

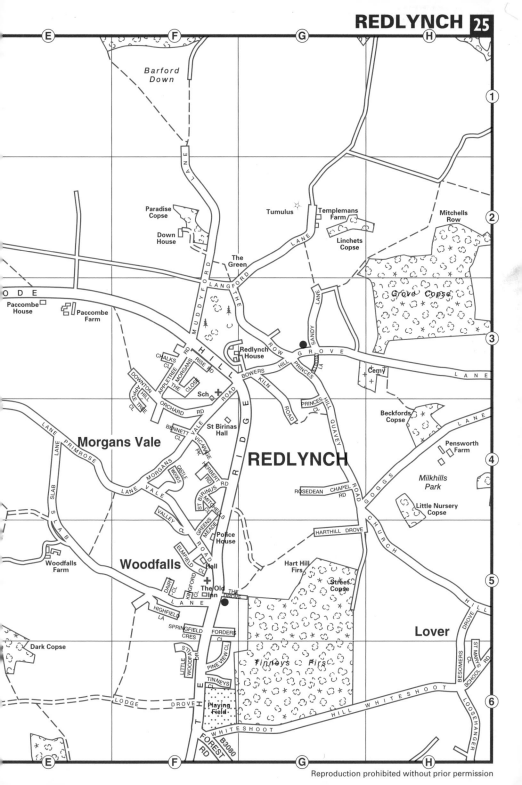

Reproduction prohibited without prior permission

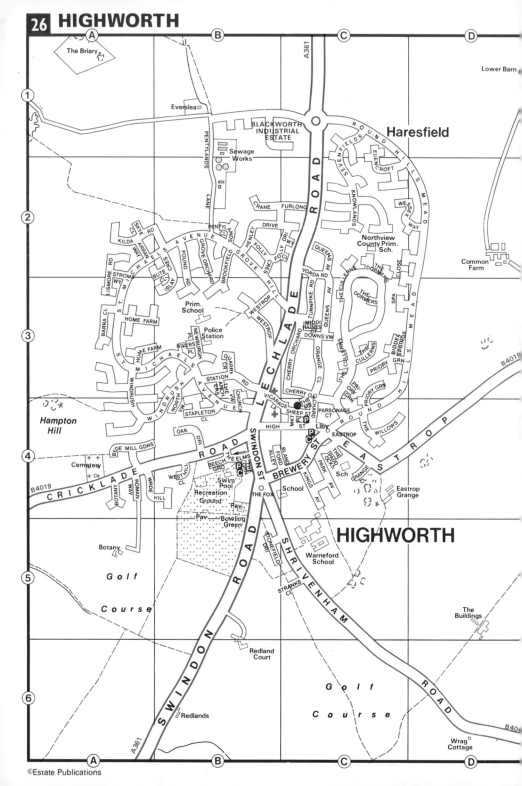

The Briary

Lower Barn

Everslea

BLACKWORTH
INDUSTRIAL
ESTATE

Haresfield

Sewage
Works

PENTYLANDS LANE

ROUND HILLS MEAD

SEVENFIELDS

EDEN CROFT

KNOWLANDS

WESSEX WAY

CRANE FURLONG

HENLEY DRIVE

FOLLY CRES

PENTYL CL

DRIVE

GROVE ORCHARD

BROOMFIELD

GROVE HILL

QUEENS AV

VORDA RD

Northview
County Prim.
Sch.

THE DORMERS

THE CULLERNS

Common
Farm

SKYE RD

ARRAN WAY

KILDA

AVENUE

POUND RD

BUTE CL

ISLAY

CRES

ST. CHAD

LISMORE RD

STROMA WY

BARRA CL

ST. MICHAELS

HOME FARM

HOME FARM

WINDRUSH

NORTH VW

NEWBURGH PL

RIVERS CL

Prim.
School

Police
Station

WESTROP

WESTROP

WESTROP

CHERRY ORCHARD

MIDDLE HAINES

DOWNS VW

ORANGE CL

QUEENS AV

TURNPIKE RD

THE CULLERNS

THE CULLERNS

THE DORMERS

SPA CLOSE

PRIORY

BIDDER SPRINGS

PRIORY GRN

THE PRIORY GRN

ROUND HILLS MEAD

Hampton
Hill

STAPLETON CL

QUARRY RD

THE ARCH VW

CHURCH

STATION RD

VICARAGE LA

SHEEP ST

HIGH ST

MKT PL

CHERRY ORCHARD

PARSONAGE CT

EASTROP

THE WILLOWS

EASTROP

OAK DRI

BDE MILL GDNS

Cemetery

BOTANY

ROMAN WAY

WRDE HILL

CRICKLADE ROAD

B4019

WEST HILL CL

BEECH GRO

THE ELMS

SWINDON ST

ROAD

SWIM
POOL

Recreation
Ground

THE FOX

BLAND FORD ALLEY

KINGS AV

PARK AV

BREWERY ST

Lib

P

School

THE ROCKS

GRANGE CL

Sch

B4019

Eastrop
Grange

Botany

Pav

Pav

Bowling
Green

Warneford
School

HIGHWORTH

Golf

Course

STONEFIELD DRI

SHRIVENHAM

STRANKS CL

Redland
Court

The
Buildings

Golf

Course

SWINDON ROAD

A361

Redlands

Wrag
Cottage

B40

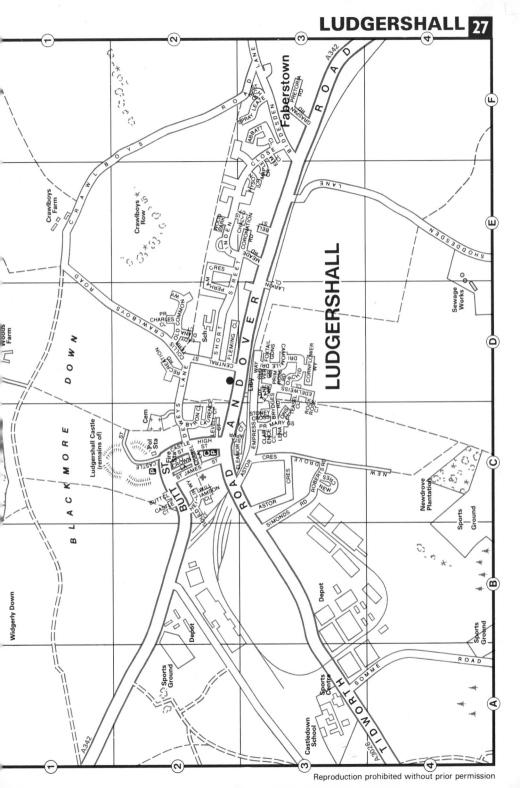

Reproduction prohibited without prior permission

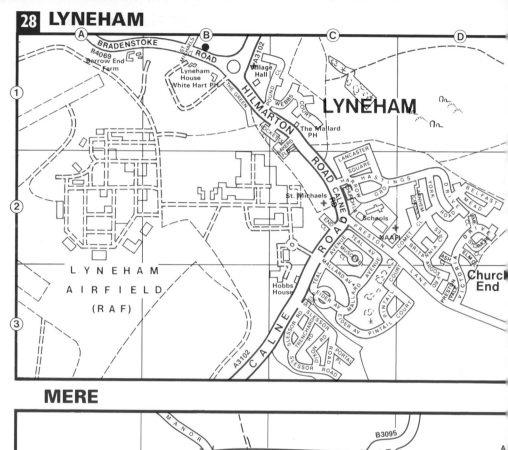

MERE

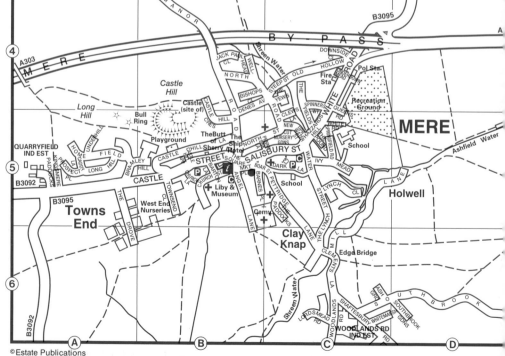

© Estate Publications

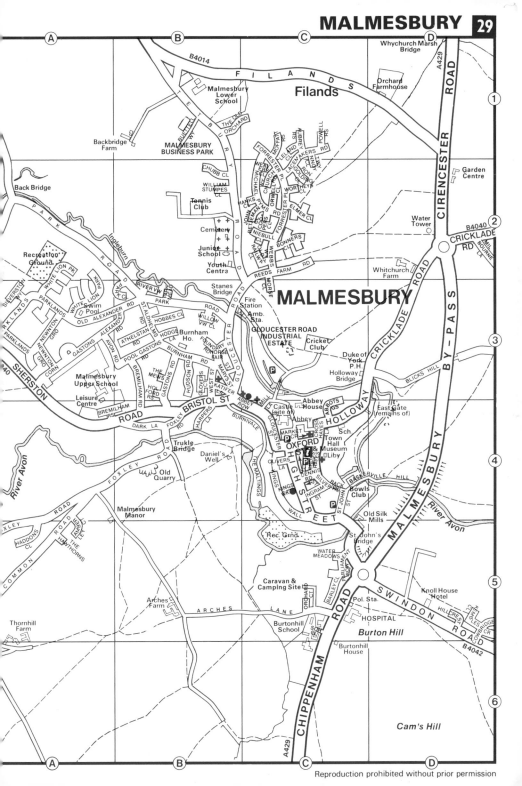

Whychurch Marsh Bridge

B4014

FILANDS

Filands

Orchard Farmhouse

CIRCENCESTER ROAD

A429

Malmesbury Lower School

THE OLD ORCHARD

Backbridge Farm

MALMESBURY BUSINESS PARK

Garden Centre

MOFFATT

ABBEY

POWELL RD

FORRESTER PL

CLEWMAKERS RD

LACKHAM RD

CHUBB CL

WEST

ALLAND

KINLLY

WORTHEY CL

Back Bridge

WILLIAM STUMPES

MICHAEL PIMS

CHURCH

ORWELL RD

FORRESTER

ELMER CL

Water Tower

Tennis Club

HANKS

BETTY

PEGGY

RD

Water Tower

PARK ROAD

Ingleburn

INVERSTON

SILVER

RKLANDS

Cemetery

NIEBUL

WEBBS

BONNERS

CRICKLADE RD

RD

Junior School

RAILWAY

Whitchurch Farm

Youth Centre

REEDS FARM RD

MORFE

B4040

CRICKLADE

Recreation Ground

WHITE LION PK

WHITE LION PK

RIVER VW

PARK

Stanes Bridge

MALMESBURY

WHITE LION

Swim Pool

RIVER VW

Fire Station

B4040

Parklands

OLD ALEXANDER RD

ST ALDHELMS

HOBBES CL

Amb. Sta.

Cricket Club

BY-PASS

NEWNTON GRO

GASTONS

ALEXANDER RD

WILLOW VW CL

GLOUCESTER ROAD INDUSTRIAL ESTATE

BLICKS HILL

PARKLANDS

CORN

AVON RD

ATHELSTAN RD

POOL GASTONS

HODGE

Burnham Ho.

FOUNDRY

HORSE FAIR

Duke of York P.H.

Holloway Bridge

SHERSTON

Malmesbury Upper School

THE MEWS

GASTONS RD

BURNHAM RD

HUDSOM RD

BURNHAM

GLOVERS

WEST ST

MARSH

WEATIFER

Abbey House

ABBOTS

East Gate (remains of)

River Avon

Leisure Centre

BREMILHAM RD

HOL GASTONS RD

DARK LA

FOXLEY RD

HARPERS LA

BRISTOL ST

BURNIVALE

Castle (site of)

Abbey

GLOUCESTER

CROSS

HOLLOWAY

Sch

MALMESBURY

ROAD

Trukle Bridge

FOXLEY ROAD

Daniel's Well

THE MALTINGS

OXFORD ST

MARKET CR

HIGH

Town Hall

Museum

Liby

BASKERVILLE HILL

River Avon

River Avon

Old Quarry

OLIVERS

P.O.

BENNIS

Bowls Club

FOXLEY

Malmesbury Manor

KINGS

WALL

BACK

ST JOHN

SILVER

INGRAM ST

STREET

Old Silk Mills

XLEY

HADDONS CL

THE HAWTHORNS

Rec. Grnd.

ST JOHNS

BARLEY CL

St John's Bridge

Knoll House Hotel

COMMON

ROAD

Caravan & Camping Site

Water Meadows

PARLIAMENT

SWINDON ROAD

HILLIERS

KNOLL CR

Arches Farm

ARCHES

LANE

ORCHARD CT

Pol. Sta.

HOSPITAL

HIGHBRIDGE CR

Thornhill Farm

Burtonhill School

CHIPPENHAM

A429

ROAD

Burton Hill

B4042

Burtonhill House

Cam's Hill

Reproduction prohibited without prior permission

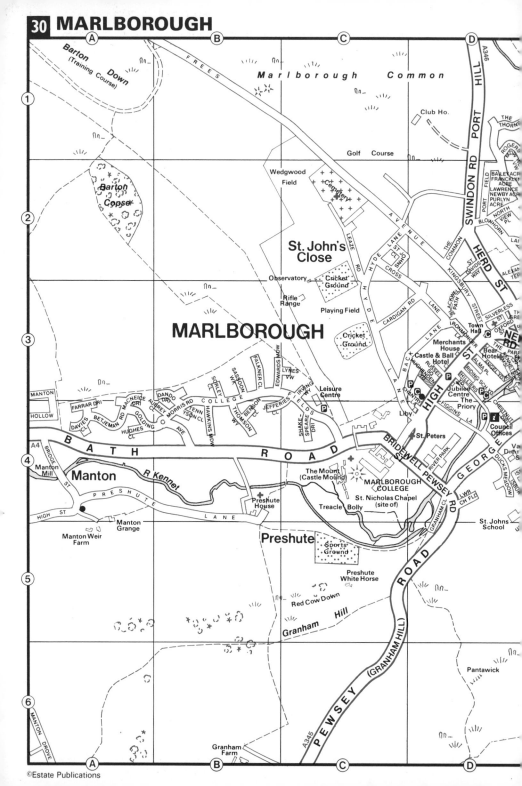

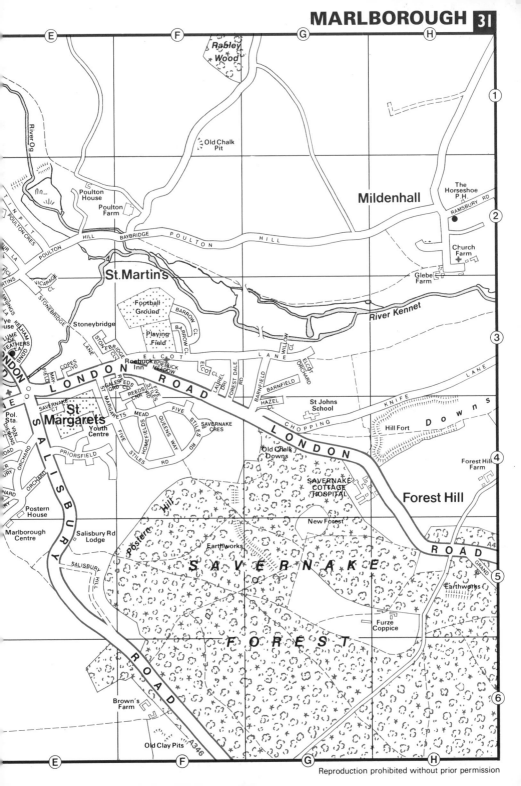

Rabley Wood

Old Chalk Pit

Mildenhall

The Horseshoe P.H.

River Og

Poulton House

Poulton Farm

RAMSBURY RD

Church Farm

HILL BAYBRIDGE POULTON HILL

Glebe Farm

St.Martins

Football Ground

River Kennet

Stoneybridge

Playing Field

BARROW CL

VICARAGE CL

STONEBRIDGE LANE

ELCOT LANE

WILLOW CL

ELCOT ORCHARD

Roebuck Inn

ROEBUCK MEADOW

COPES YD

REEDS GRD

FIVE STILES

FOREST DALE RD

BARNFIELD

BARNFIELD

KNIFE

LANE

Downs

St Johns School

CHOPPING

Hill Fort

LONDON ROAD

St Margarets

SAVERNAKE CT

Youth Centre

QUEENS WAY

HOMEFIELDS

MEAD

FIVE STILES RD

SAVERNAKE CRES

HAZEL CL

Old Chalk Downs

LONDON ROAD

Forest Hill Farm

Pol. Sta.

POSTMANS

PRIORSFIELD

FIVE STILES

SAVERNAKE COTTAGE HOSPITAL

Forest Hill

Postern Hill

New Forest

A4

ORCHARD

Postern House

Marlborough Centre

Salisbury Rd Lodge

Earthworks

SAVERNAKE

ROAD

GRAND

Earthworks

SALISBURY

ROAD

Furze Coppice

FOREST

Brown's Farm

Old Clay Pits

A346

Reproduction prohibited without prior permission

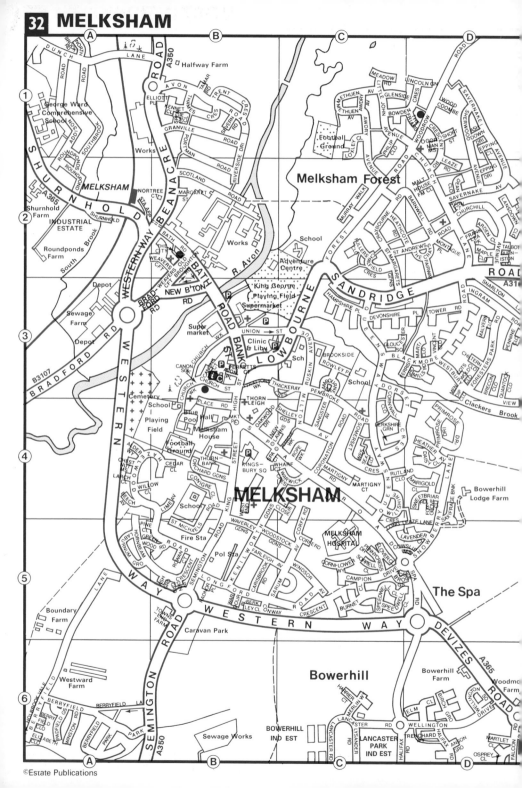

©Estate Publications

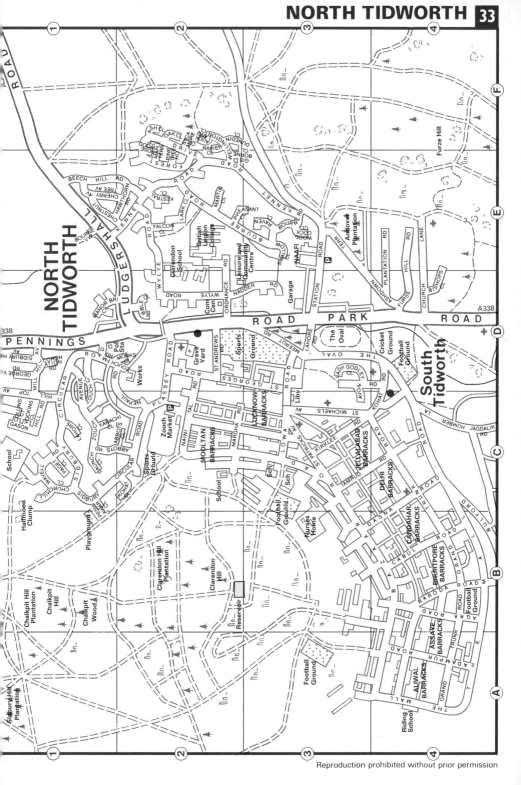

Reproduction prohibited without prior permission

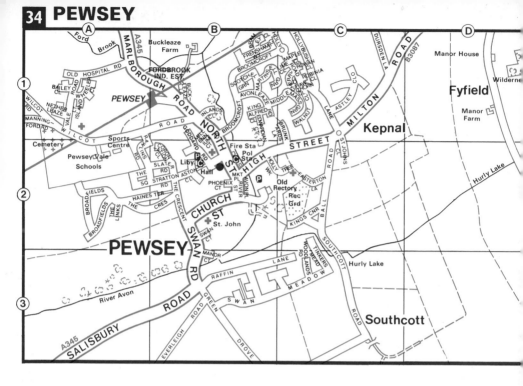

POTTERNE

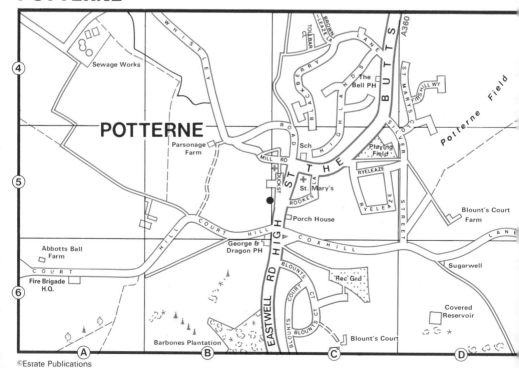

©Estate Publications

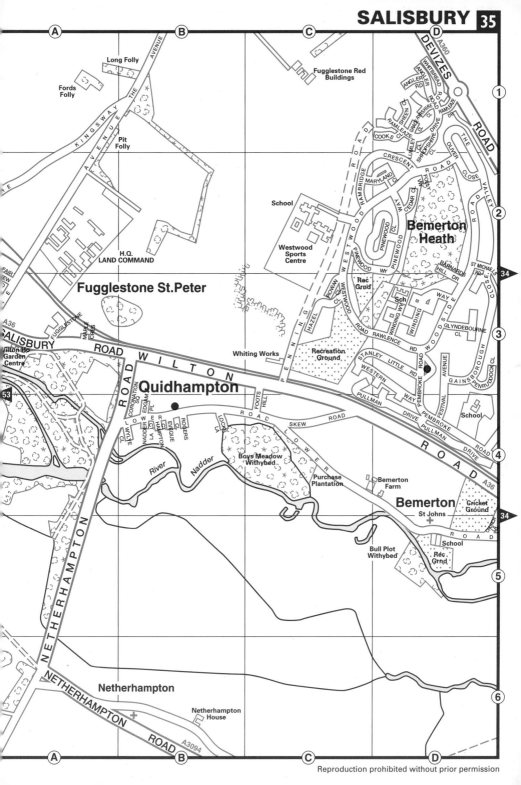

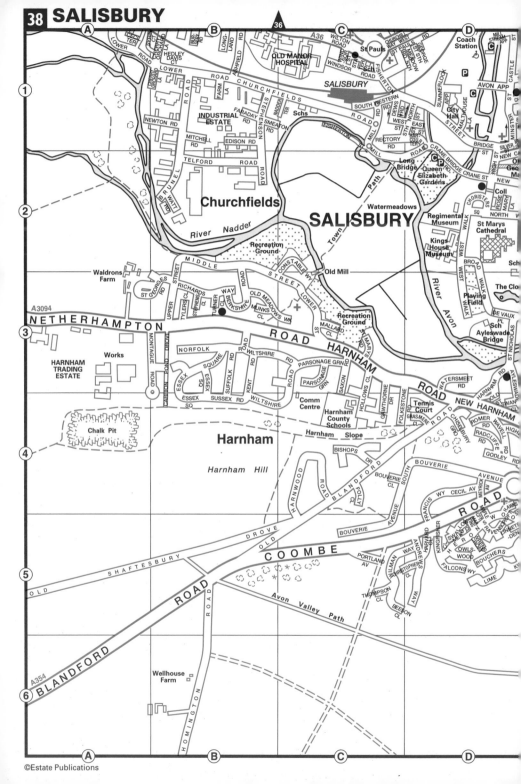

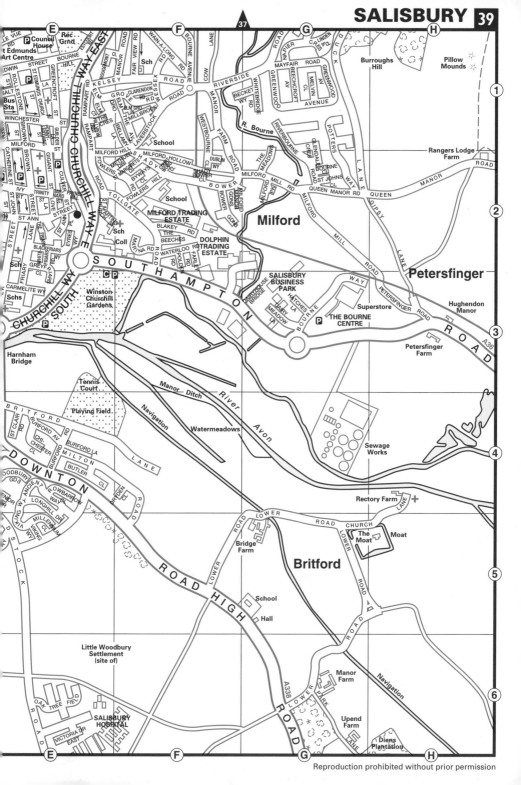

Reproduction prohibited without prior permission

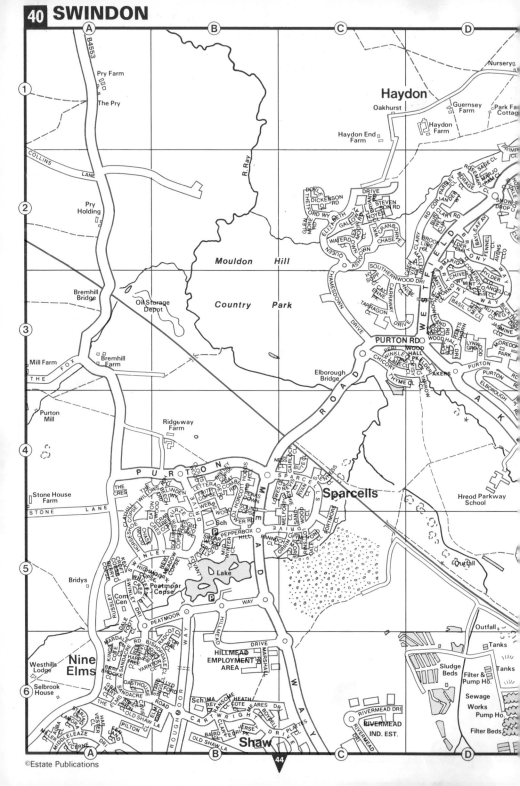

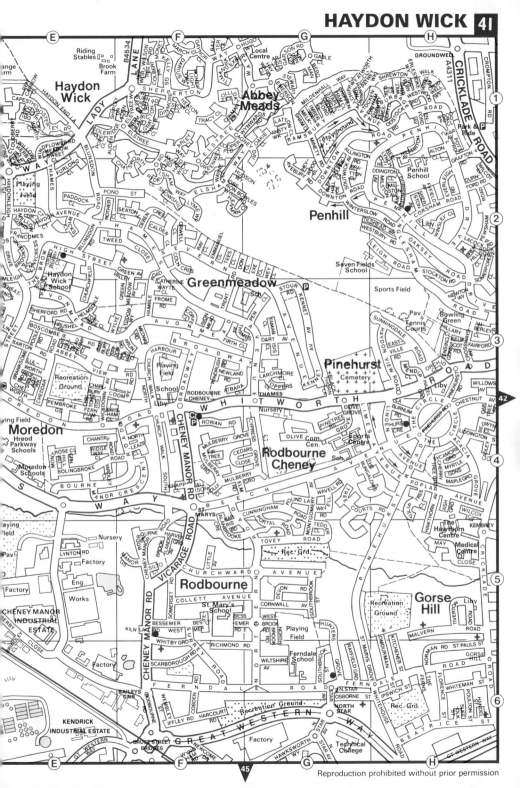

Reproduction prohibited without prior permission

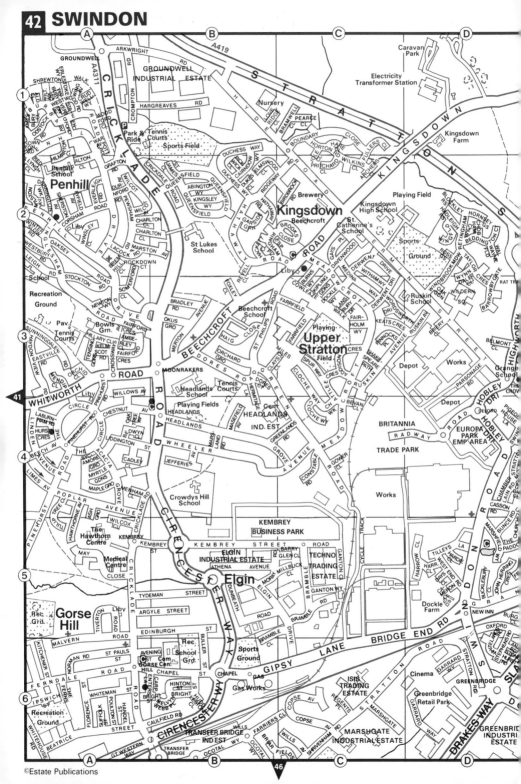

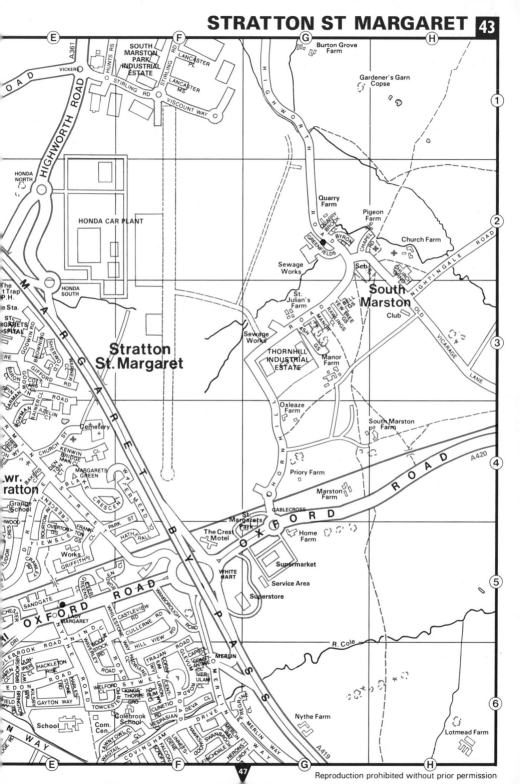

South Marston Park Industrial Estate

Burton Grove Farm

Gardener's Garn Copse

Honda North

Honda Car Plant

Honda South

Quarry Farm

Pigeon Farm

Church Farm

Greenfields

Sewage Works

St. Julian's Farm

South Marston

Club

Stratton St. Margaret

Thornhill Industrial Estate

Manor Farm

Sewage Works

Oxleaze Farm

Cemetery

South Marston Farm

Priory Farm

Marston Farm

Grange School

St. Margarets Park

Gablecross

The Crest Motel

Home Farm

Works

White Hart

Supermarket

Lady Margaret

Service Area

Superstore

OXFORD ROAD

Colebrook School

School

Com. Cen.

R. Cole

Nythe Farm

Lotmead Farm

Reproduction prohibited without prior permission

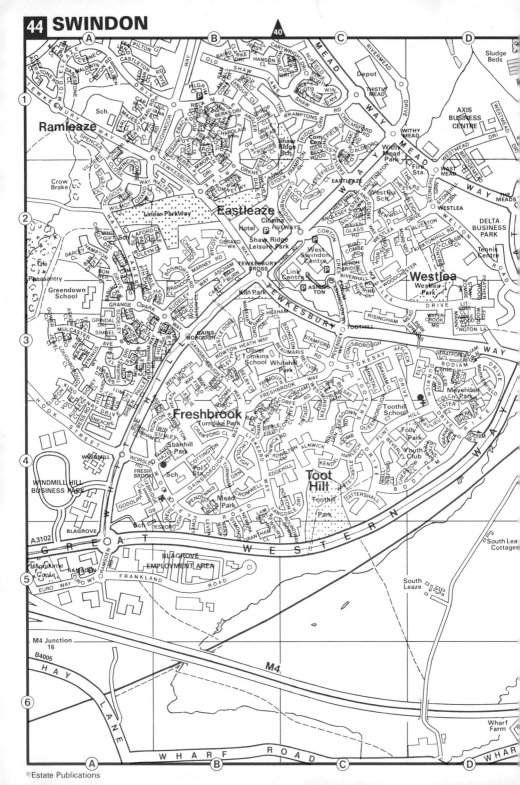

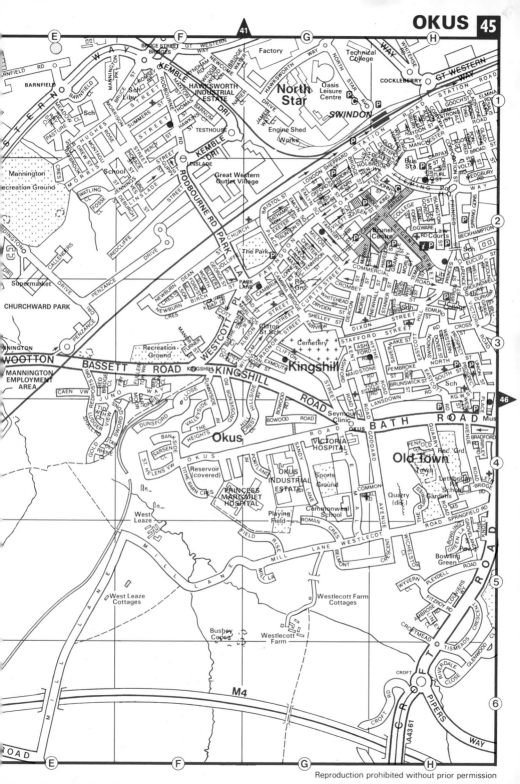

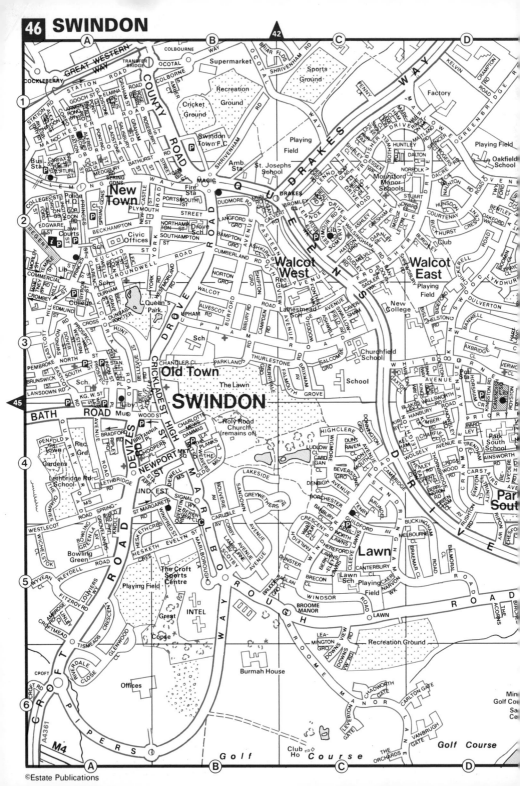

©Estate Publications

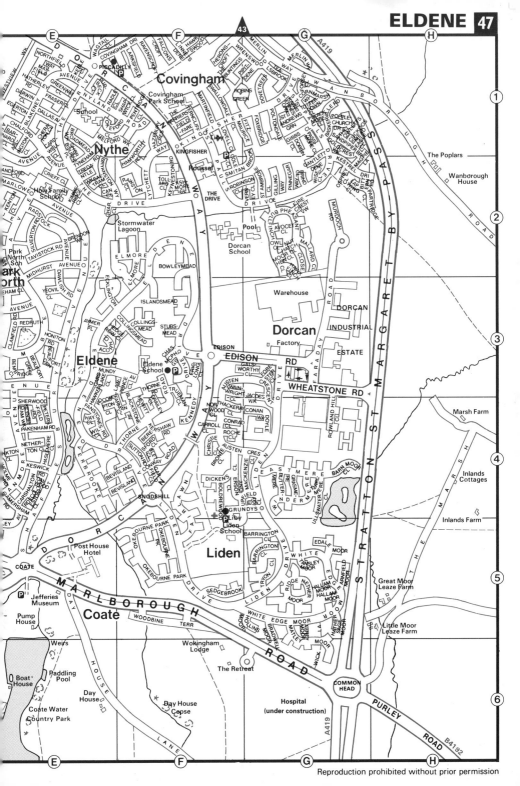

Reproduction prohibited without prior permission

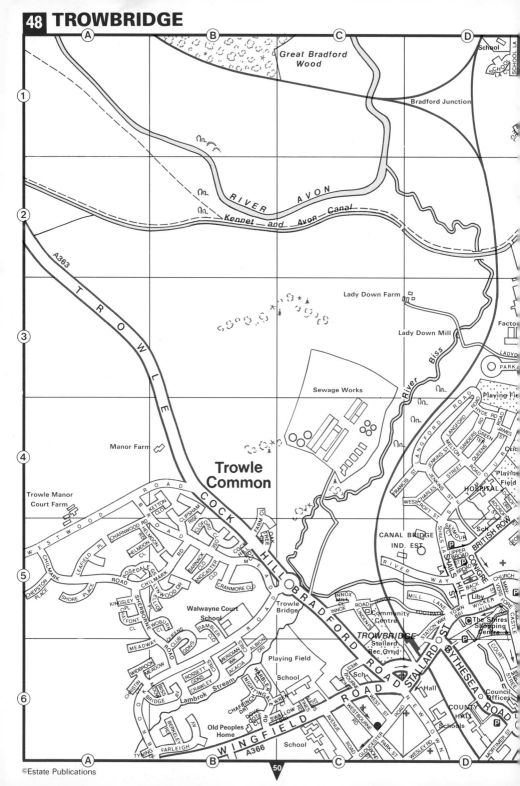

©Estate Publications

Hilperton Marsh Farm

Hilperton Marsh

Hilperton

Church Farm

Police House

Hall Playing Field

Lion & Fiddle PH

Palmers Close

TROWBRIDGE

The Paddocks

Fire Sta

Amb Sta

Trowbridge Rugby Club

Trowbridge Lodge Residential Park

Paxcroft Brook

Cemetery

School

Depot

Warehouse

Warehouse

Basin

Swan Dri Marina

W.C.C. Consortium

The Park

Youth Centre

Civic Hall

Supermarket

Reproduction prohibited without prior permission

©Estate Publications

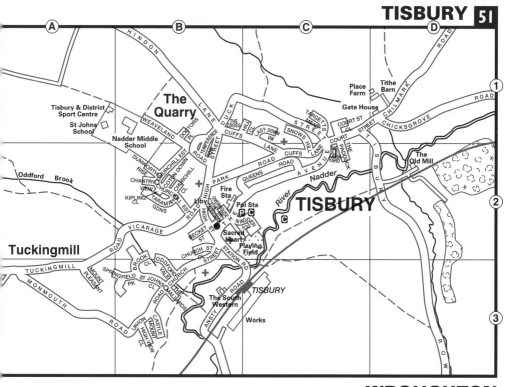

TISBURY

The Quarry

Tuckingmill

Tisbury & District Sport Centre
St Johns School
Nadder Middle School
Oddford Brook
Place Farm
Tithe Barn
Gate House
Court St
The Old Mill
Fire Sta
Pol Sta
Sacred Heart
Playing Field
The South Western
Works
River Nadder

WROUGHTON

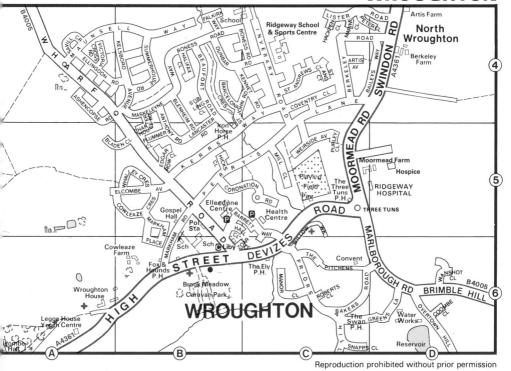

Ridgeway School & Sports Centre
Artis Farm
North Wroughton
Berkeley Farm
School
Lister
Swindon Rd
Moormead Rd
Moormead Farm
Hospice
Ridgeway Hospital
Three Tuns P.H.
The Three Tuns
Iron Horse P.H.
Playing Field Pav
Ellendune Centre
Health Centre
Gospel Hall
Pol Sta
Liby
Cowleaze Farm
Fox & Hounds P.H.
The Ely P.H.
Convent
Washot Cl
Brimble Hill
Wroughton House
Brook Meadow Caravan Park
The Swan P.H.
Water Works
Legge House Youth Centre
Reservoir

WROUGHTON

Reproduction prohibited without prior permission

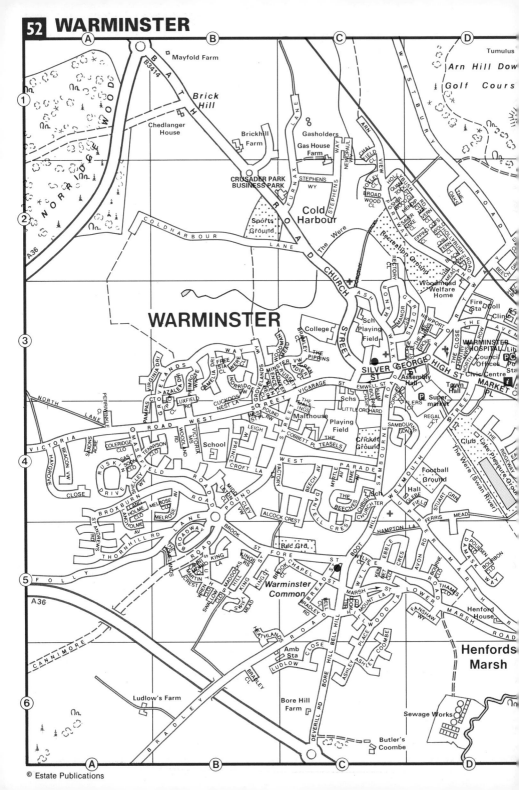

52 WARMINSTER

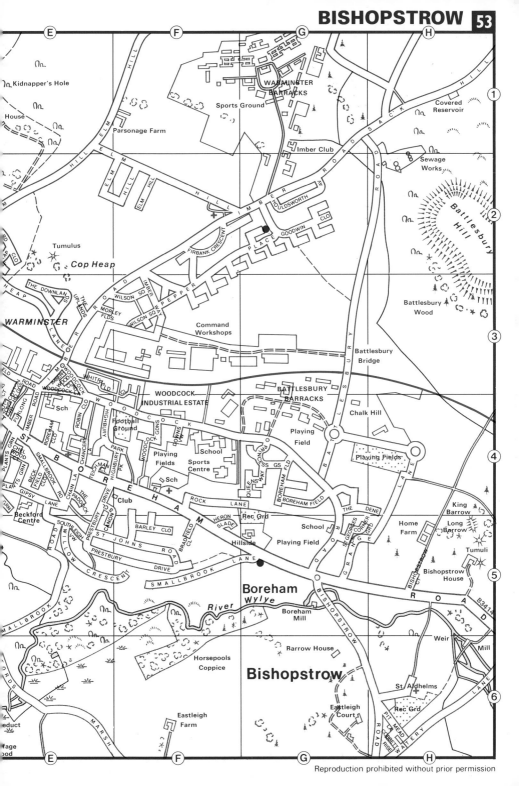

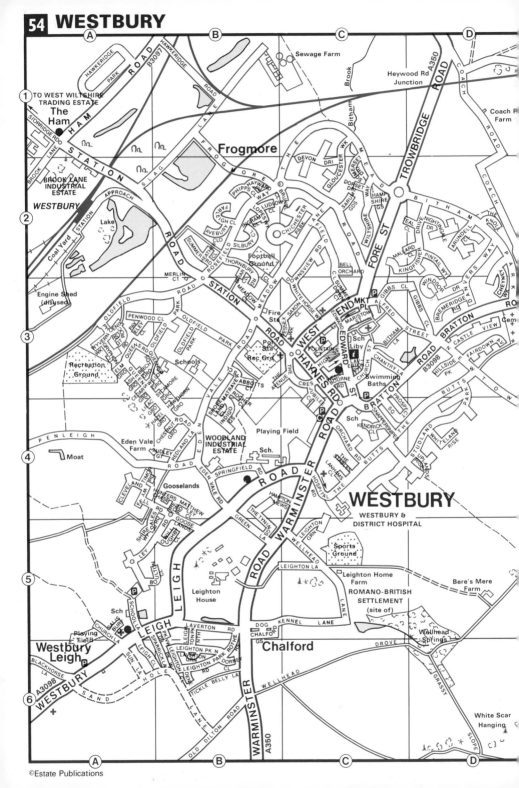

©Estate Publications

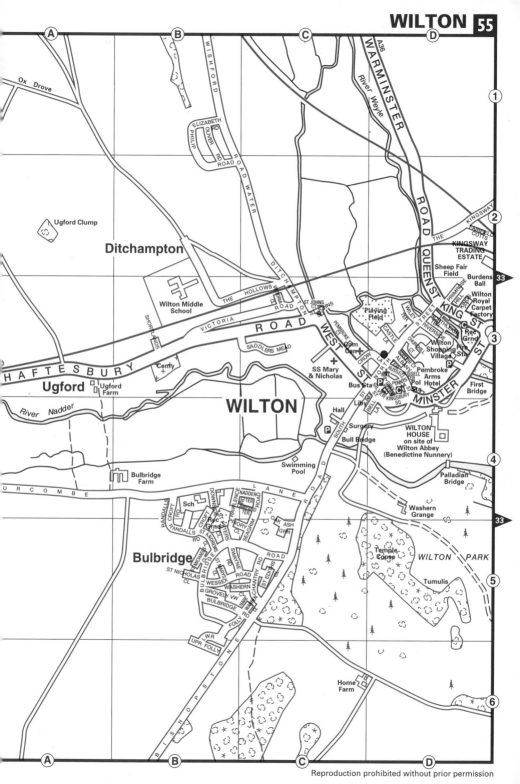

Reproduction prohibited without prior permission

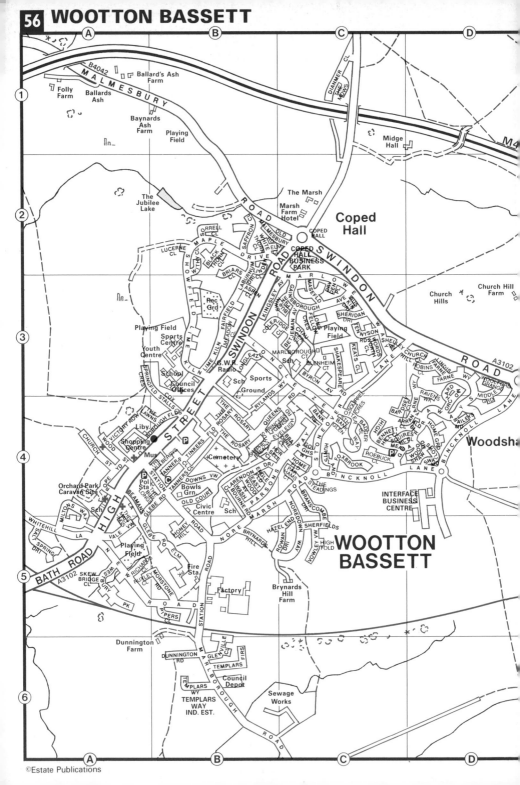

WOOTTON BASSETT

Coped Hall

Woodsh...

©Estate Publications

The Index includes some names for which there is insufficient space on the maps. These names are preceded by an * and are followed by the nearest adjoining thoroughfare.

ALDBOURNE

Alma Rd. SN8 — 12 B1
Back La. SN8 — 12 B2
Castle St. SN8 — 12 A2
Chandlers La. SN8 — 12 B3
Claridge Clo. SN8 — 12 B3
Cook Clo. SN8 — 12 B1
Cook Rd. SN8 — 12 B1
Crooked Corner. SN8 — 12 B2
Farm La. SN8 — 12 B2
Glebe Clo. SN8 — 12 B2
Goddards La. SN8 — 12 B2
Grasshills. SN8 — 12 B1
Hawkins Rd. SN8 — 12 B3
Hillwood Rd. SN8 — 12 A3
Kandahar. SN8 — 12 B1
Lottage Rd. SN8 — 12 B1
Lottage Way. SN8 — 12 B1
Marlborough Rd. SN8 — 12 B2
Oxford St. SN8 — 12 B2
Rectory Wood. SN8 — 12 B3
St Michaels Clo. SN8 — 12 B2
South St. SN8 — 12 B2
Southfield. SN8 — 12 B3
Southward La. SN8 — 12 B3
Stock La. SN8 — 12 A3
The Butts. SN8 — 12 B3
The Downs. SN8 — 12 B3
The Garlings. SN8 — 12 B3
The Green. SN8 — 12 B2
The Knoll. SN8 — 12 B1
The Paddocks. SN8 — 12 B2
The Square. SN8 — 12 B2
Turnpike. SN8 — 12 B2
West St. SN8 — 12 A2
Westfield Chase. SN8 — 12 A2
Whitley Rd. SN8 — 12 A3
Windmill Clo. SN8 — 12 B1

AMESBURY

Abbess Clo. SP4 — 13 C3
Abbey La. SP4 — 13 C3
Abbey Sq. SP4 — 13 B2
Alanbrooke Clo. SP4 — 13 C1
Allington Way. SP4 — 13 E3
Amesbury By Pass. SP4 — 13 A1
Amesbury Rd. SP4 — 13 F3
Annets Clo. SP4 — 13 D1
Antrobus Rd. SP4 — 13 C2
Aragon Clo. SP4 — 13 D1
Ashley Walk. SP4 — 13 E3
Avon Bldgs. SP4 — 13 C2
Avonstoke Clo. SP4 — 13 C3
Barnes Wallis Clo. SP4 — 13 F3
Bawdsey Rd. SP4 — 13 E4
Beacon Clo. SP4 — 13 D1
Beamont Way. SP4 — 13 E1
Beauchamp Dri. SP4 — 13 E2
Beaulieu Rd. SP4 — 13 D3
Beger Rd. SP4 — 13 E4
Blackcross Rd. SP4 — 13 F3
Boscombe Down Rd. SP4 — 13 D2
Bramley Way. SP4 — 13 D2
Buckland Ct. SP4 — 13 C3
Burwood Rd. SP4 — 13 F3
Butterfield Dri. SP4 — 13 E2
Cadnam Cres. SP4 — 13 F3
Canbury Clo. SP4 — 13 F3
Carleon Clo. SP4 — 13 E2
Carleton Pl. SP4 — 13 C2
Chambers Av. SP4 — 13 E1
Cherrytree Way. SP4 — 13 D2
Chesterfield Clo. SP4 — 13 F2
Church La. SP4 — 13 C2
Church St. SP4 — 13 B2

Coach House Mews. SP4 — 13 C2
Cold Harbour. SP4 — 13 C2
Coltsfoot Clo. SP4 — 13 D2
Coniston Clo. SP4 — 13 F2
Countess Rd. SP4 — 13 B1
Cranleigh Clo. SP4 — 13 F2
Darrell Rd. SP4 — 13 D1
Dawbeny Dri. SP4 — 13 E2
Devereux Rd. SP4 — 13 D2
Diddledown Rd. SP4 — 13 E3
Earls Clo. SP4 — 13 F3
Earls Court Rd. SP4 — 13 C2
Edwards Rd. SP4 — 13 C2
Evergreen Way. SP4 — 13 D3
Fairfax Clo. SP4 — 13 C2
Finnis Rd. SP4 — 13 D2
Flitcroft. SP4 — 13 D3
Flower La. SP4 — 13 B2
Fosters Bushes. SP4 — 13 E2
Gauntlet Rd. SP4 — 13 C2
Geneville Rise. SP4 — 13 E3
Hamilton Clo. SP4 — 13 F3
Harvard Way. SP4 — 13 E3
Haywain. SP4 — 13 D3
Heyford Clo. SP4 — 13 F3
High St. SP4 — 13 B2
Highfield Rd. SP4 — 13 D2
Hillview Clo. SP4 — 13 C1
Holders Rd. SP4 — 13 D2
Hudson Rd. SP4 — 13 D2
Hurley Clo. SP4 — 13 F2
Imber Av. SP4 — 13 E3
INDUSTRIAL & RETAIL:
Amesbury Ind Est. SP4 — 13 D1
Boscombe Down Business Park. SP4 — 13 E1
Jaggard View. SP4 — 13 D3
James Rd. SP4 — 13 D1
Javelin Clo. SP4 — 13 E3
John Gay Rd. SP4 — 13 D2
Kickdom Clo. SP4 — 13 E3
Kitchener Rd. SP4 — 13 C2
Lanes Clo. SP4 — 13 D2
Lanfear Clo. SP4 — 13 D2
Lawrence Clo. SP4 — 13 D3
Leonard Cheshire Clo. SP4 — 13 E3
Lightning Rd. SP4 — 13 E3
London Rd. SP4 — 13 C2
Lords Croft. SP4 — 13 C1
Lumley Walk. SP4 — 13 E3
Lynchets Rd. SP4 — 13 C3
Lynchfield Rd. SP4 — 13 D3
Lyndhurst Rd. SP4 — 13 D3
McKie Rd. SP4 — 13 E3
Main Rd. SP4 — 13 F3
Martlesham Rd. SP4 — 13 E4
Melor Vw. SP4 — 13 D3
Millgreen Rd. SP4 — 13 D3
Mills Way. SP4 — 13 E1
Milton Rd. SP4 — 13 E3
Moyne Gdns. SP4 — 13 E3
Nicolson Clo. SP4 — 13 F2
North Rd. SP4 — 13 F3
Nursery Clo. SP4 — 13 C2
Oak Pl. SP4 — 13 D1
Old Granary La. SP4 — 13 C2
Orchard Way. SP4 — 13 D2
Orford Rd. SP4 — 13 E4
Pains Way. SP4 — 13 D3
Parsonage Rd. SP4 — 13 C3
Pilots Vw. SP4 — 13 E3
Porton Rd. SP4 — 13 E3
Purvis Clo. SP4 — 13 F2
Queensberry Rd. SP4 — 13 D1
Raleigh Cres. SP4 — 13 E2
Ratfyn Rd. SP4 — 13 C1
Recreation Rd. SP4 — 13 B3
Ringwood Av. SP4 — 13 D3
Riverside Av. SP4 — 13 A2
Robbins Ridge. SP4 — 13 D3
Romsey Rd. SP4 — 13 E1
St Annes Clo. SP4 — 13 D2
Salisbury Rd, Amesbury. SP4 — 13 C2
Salisbury Rd, Boscombe Down. SP4 — 13 F4
Salisbury St. SP4 — 13 B2

School La. SP4 — 13 C2
Simmance Way. SP4 — 13 D2
Smithfield St. SP4 — 13 C2
Solstice Rise. SP4 — 13 C2
South Mill Clo. SP4 — 13 C3
South Mill Rd. SP4 — 13 C3
Southmill Hill. SP4 — 13 C4
Station Cotts. SP4 — 13 D1
Stockbarrow. SP4 — 13 D3
Stonehenge Rd. SP4 — 13 A2
Tanners Field. SP4 — 13 E3
Tempest Rd. SP4 — 13 E3
The Centre. SP4 — 13 C2
The Drove. SP4 — 13 C2
Thurlow Clo. SP4 — 13 F3
Tisbury Rd. SP4 — 13 E1
Tuckers Clo. SP4 — 13 D3
Underwood Dri. SP4 — 13 E3
Vernon Clo. SP4 — 13 F2
Verny Clo. SP4 — 13 E2
Virginia Clo. SP4 — 13 F2
Westland Clo. SP4 — 13 F2
Whelan Way. SP4 — 13 E2
Wilcot Clo. SP4 — 13 F3
Winchester Clo. SP4 — 13 A2
Wittenham Vw. SP4 — 13 D3

AVEBURY

Beckhampton Rd. SN8 — 12 A6
Bray St. SN8 — 12 A5
Frog La. SN8 — 12 B6
High St. SN8 — 12 C5
Nash Rd. SN8 — 12 A6
South St. SN8 — 12 A6
Swindon Rd. SN8 — 12 C4
Truslow Cottages. SN8 — 12 A6
West Kennet Av. SN8 — 12 D5

BRADFORD-ON-AVON

Ancliff Sq. BA15 — 14 B5
Ashley Clo. BA15 — 15 E1
Ashley La. BA15 — 14 C2
Ashley Rd. BA15 — 15 E1
Avon Clo. BA15 — 15 G3
Avonfield Av. BA15 — 15 G4
Baileys Barn. BA15 — 15 F4
Bainton Clo. BA15 — 15 G2
Bancroft. BA15 — 15 G1
Barn Piece. BA15 — 15 G5
Barton Orchard. BA15 — 15 E3
Bassetts Pasture. BA15 — 15 F5
Bath Rd. BA15 — 15 F1
Bear Clo. BA15 — 15 F1
Bearfield Bldgs. BA15 — 15 F1
Beddoe Clo. BA15 — 15 G5
Belcombe Pl. BA15 — 15 E3
Belcombe Rd. BA15 — 15 E3
Berryfield Rd. BA15 — 15 F2
Bobbin La. BA15 — 14 B5
Bobbin Pk. BA15 — 14 C6
Boswell Rd. BA15 — 14 B6
Bradford Rd. BA15 — 14 A3
Bridge St. BA15 — 15 F3
Brookwood. BA15 — 14 B2
Broomground. BA15 — 14 B2
Budbury Clo. BA15 — 15 E2
Budbury Circ. BA15 — 15 E2
Budbury Pl. BA15 — 15 E2
Budbury Ridge. BA15 — 15 E2
Budbury Tyning. BA15 — 15 E2
Bull Pit. BA15 — 15 F3
Cedar Ct. BA15 — 15 F1
Cemetery La. BA15 — 15 H2
Chestnut Gro. BA15 — 15 H2
Christchurch Rd. BA15 — 15 F1
Church Acre. BA15 — 15 E2
Church St. BA15 — 15 F3
Churches. BA15 — 15 E2
Conigre Hill. BA15 — 15 E2
Coppice Hill. BA15 — 15 F2
Coronation Av. BA15 — 15 F2
Cottles La. BA15 — 14 B3
Crown Ct. BA15 — 15 H2

Culver Rd. BA15 — 15 G4
Dane Clo. BA15 — 14 B2
Dane Rise. BA15 — 14 A2
Deverell Clo. BA15 — 15 G5
Downavon. BA15 — 15 G4
Downs Clo. BA15 — 15 E2
Downs View. BA15 — 15 F2
Druces Hill. BA15 — 15 F2
Elmfield. BA15 — 15 E2
Elms Cross.BA15 — 15 E6
Elms Cross Dri. BA15 — 15 F4
Fairleigh View. BA15 — 14 B6
Fieldins. BA15 — 15 E3
Fitzmaurice Clo. BA15 — 15 G5
Fitzmaurice Pl. BA15 — 15 F4
Follyfield. BA15 — 15 G5
Frenchgrass. BA15 — 15 G3
Friary Clo. BA15 — 14 B5
Frome Rd. BA15 — 15 F3
Grange View. BA15 — 15 G2
Great Orchard. BA15 — 14 B5
Green La. BA15 — 14 B3
Greenland Mills. BA15 — 15 G3
Greenland View. BA15 — 15 G3
Grove Leaze. BA15 — 15 E3
Hare Knapp. BA15 — 15 E3
Hebden Rd. BA15 — 15 H5
Highfield Rd. BA15 — 15 G2
Hob House Clo. BA15 — 15 G5
Holly Bush Clo. BA15 — 14 B2
Horton Clo. BA15 — 15 G5
Huntingdon Pl. BA15 — 15 F2
Huntingdon Rise. BA15 — 15 E1
Huntingdon St. BA15 — 15 F1
Iford La. BA15 — 14 A6
INDUSTRIAL & RETAIL:
Elmscros Shopping Centre & Business Pk. BA15 — 15 E5
Treenwood Ind Est. BA15 — 15 F5
Ivy Ter. BA15 — 15 F2
John Rennie Clo. BA15 — 15 G5
Jones Hill. BA15 — 15 E4
Junction Rd. BA15 — 15 F3
Kennet Gdns. BA15 — 15 F4
King Alfred Way. BA15 — 14 A2
Kingsfield. BA15 — 15 G2
Kingsfield Clo. BA15 — 15 G2
Kingsfield Grange Rd. BA15 — 15 G2
Kingston Av. BA15 — 15 G2
Kingston Rd. BA15 — 15 F3
Late Broads. BA15 — 14 A2
Leigh Park Rd. BA15 — 15 G1
Leigh Rd. BA15 — 15 G1
Leslie Rise. BA15 — 14 C6
Limpley Stoke Rd. BA15 — 14 A2
Linden Cres. BA15 — 14 C6
Lindisfarne Clo. BA15 — 14 B2
Lister Gro. BA15 — 14 C6
Lodden Way. BA15 — 14 A2
Lyddieth Ct. BA15 — 14 A2
Magnon Rd. BA15 — 15 F2
Market St. BA15 — 15 F2
Masons La. BA15 — 15 E2
Meadowfield. BA15 — 15 E3
Methuen Clo. BA15 — 15 G5
Middle Rank. BA15 — 15 F2
Mill La. BA15 — 15 F3
Millbourn Clo. BA15 — 14 A2
Moulton Dri. BA15 — 15 F5
Mount Pleasant. BA15 — 15 F2
Mythern Mdw. BA15 — 15 G4
New Rd. BA15 — 15 G2
Newtown. BA15 — 15 E3
Northfield. BA15 — 15 F1
Orchard Clo. BA15 — 14 C6
Orchard Gdns. BA15 — 15 F1
Palairet Clo. BA15 — 15 F4
Palmer Dri. BA15 — 15 G1
Peto Gro. BA15 — 14 C6
Piplar Ground. BA15 — 15 F5
Poston Way. BA15 — 14 A2
Poulton. BA15 — 15 G4
Poulton La. BA15 — 15 H2
Pound La. BA15 — 15 F3
Priory Clo. BA15 — 15 F2
Priory Park. BA15 — 15 F2
Quarry Clo. BA3 — 14 A3

Regents Pl. BA15 — 15 F3
Rickfield. BA15 — 15 E3
River Ct. BA15 — 15 F3
Rosemary Steps. BA15 — 15 F2
Rosemary Wk. BA15 — 15 F3
Rowden La. BA15 — 15 F5
St Aldhelm Rd. BA15 — 15 G4
St Katherines Quay. BA15 — 15 F4
St Laurence Rd. BA15 — 15 F3
St Margarets Hill. BA15 — 15 F3
St Margarets St. BA15 — 15 F2
St Margarets Steps. BA15 — 15 F3
St Margarets Villas. BA15 — 15 F3
St Nicholas Clo. BA15 — 14 A2
Sand Clo. BA15 — 15 G2
Sandy Leaze. BA15 — 15 F5
Saxon Way. BA15 — 14 B2
Silver St. BA15 — 15 F2
Sladesbrook. BA15 — 15 G1
Sladesbrook Clo. BA15 — 15 G2
Southleigh. BA15 — 15 E4
Southville Clo. BA15 — 15 G4
Southville Rd. BA15 — 15 G4
Southway Rd. BA15 — 15 H5
Spencers Orchard. BA15 — 15 F5
Springfield. BA15 — 15 G3
Stonefield Clo. BA15 — 15 G3
The Old Batch. BA15 — 15 E1
The Elms. BA15 — 14 E1
The Croft. BA15 — 14 C6
The Laurels. BA15 — 14 C6
The Maltings. BA15 — 15 F4
The Mead. BA15 — 15 F3
The Mill Ho. BA15 — 15 G3
The Pastures. BA15 — 14 B6
The Shambles. BA15 — 15 F2
The Wilderness. BA15 — 15 F2
Tory. BA15 — 15 E3
Tory Pl. BA15 — 15 E3
Trowbridge Rd. BA15 — 15 F3
Tyning Rd. BA15 — 14 B2
Tynings Way. BA15 — 14 C6
Upper Mill. BA15 — 15 G3
Upper Regents Park. BA15 — 15 F3
Upper Westwood. BA15 — 14 A6
Vine Cotts. BA15 — 15 F3
Wellside Mill. BA15 — 15 F3
Westfield. BA15 — 14 D2
Westwood Rd. BA15 — 14 D6
White Hill. BA15 — 15 F3
White Horse Rd. BA15 — 14 B2
Whiteheads La. BA15 — 15 F2
Widbrook Hill. BA15 — 15 H6
Widbrook Vw. BA15 — 15 G4
Wine St. BA15 — 15 E2
Wine St Ter. BA15 — 15 E2
Winsley Rd. BA15 — 15 C2
Woolley Clo. BA15 — 15 G2
Woolley Dri. BA15 — 15 G2
Woolley St. BA15 — 15 G2
Woolley Ter. BA15 — 15 G2

BULFORD/DURRINGTON

Addison Sq. SP4 — 16 B2
Alberta Gdns. SP4 — 16 F3
Andrew Clo. SP4 — 16 B2
Ann Cres. SP4 — 16 B2
Avondown Rd. SP4 — 16 C2
Birchwood Dri. SP4 — 16 C2
Bowdich Clo. SP4 — 16 C1
Bulford Driveway. SP4 — 16 E2
Bulford Droveway. SP4 — 16 D3
Bulford Hill. SP4 — 16 C3
Bulford Rd, Bulford. SP4 — 16 E2
Bulford Rd, Durrington. SP4 — 16 B1
Camellia Clo. SP4 — 16 D3
Charles Rd. SP4 — 16 D3
Church La. SP4 — 16 B1
Church St. SP4 — 16 B1
Churchill Av. SP4 — 16 D3

Clayton Rd. SP4 16 E3
College Rd. SP4 16 B1
Coronation Rd. SP4 16 B2
Countess Rd. SP4 16 A3
Crescent Rd. SP4 16 D3
Cygnet Dri. SP4 16 E3
Dorset Clo. SP4 16 E3
Double Hedges. SP4 16 D4
Downland Way. SP4 16 B1
Downleaze. SP4 16 B1
Dukes Way. SP4 16 E3
Elizabeth Rd. SP4 16 B2
Glebe Rd. SP4 16 C2
Glendale Rd. SP4 16 C2
Greenland Clo. SP4 16 B2
Hackthorn Rd. SP4 16 A1
Hampshire Clo. SP4 16 E3
Herons Walk. SP4 16 C2
High St, Bulford. SP4 16 D3
High St,
 Durrington. SP4 16 B1
John French Way. SP4 16 E3
Kingfisher Dri. SP4 16 C2
Larkhill Rd. SP4 16 A2
Latchmere Lodge. SP4 16 C2
Ledger Hill Clo. SP4 16 D3
Lily Walk. SP4 16 C2
Longfield Clo. SP4 16 B1
Mackenzie Gdns. SP4 16 F3
Maple Way. SP4 16 A1
Marina Clo. SP4 16 B2
Marina Cres. SP4 16 B2
Marina Rd. SP4 16 B2
Meadow Rd. SP4 16 E3
Meads Rd. SP4 16 B2
Milston Rd. SP4 16 D1
Milston Vw. SP4 16 C1
Netheravon Rd. SP4 16 A2
New Rd. SP4 16 B2
Newmans Way. SP4 16 E3
Old Barns Way. SP4 16 B1
Old Coach Rd. SP4 16 D3
Old Ward Rd. SP4 16 F3
Ontario Gdns. SP4 16 F3
Orchard End. SP4 16 D3
Philip Rd. SP4 16 B2
Pinckneys Way. SP4 16 A2
Poores Rd. SP4 16 C1
Recreation Rd. SP4 16 C1
Reed Walk. SP4 16 B1
Ridgmount. SP4 16 B1
River Way. SP4 16 C2
Robin Hill La. SP4 16 C2
St Leonards Clo. SP4 16 D3
Salisbury Rd. SP4 16 D4
School Dri. SP4 16 B2
School Rd. SP4 16 C1
Station Ter. SP4 16 D4
Stonehenge Rd. SP4 16 A2
Swan Clo. SP4 16 C2
Swattons Clo. SP4 16 E3
The Avenue. SP4 16 B2
The Ham. SP4 16 B1
The Leaze. SP4 16 E3
Vancouver Gdns. SP4 16 F3
Water St. SP4 16 D3
Watergate La. SP4 16 C4
Westfield Clo. SP4 16 A2
Willow Rd. SP4 16 A1
Wiltshire Clo. SP4 16 B1
Windsor Mews. SP4 16 B1
Windsor Rd. SP4 16 B2
Winnipeg Gdns. SP4 16 F3
Yew Tree Clo. SP4 16 C2

CALNE

Abberd La. SN11 17 D2
Abberd Way. SN11 17 C3
Alma Ter. SN11 17 B2
Anchor Rd. SN11 17 C3
Angell Clo. SN11 17 C3
Avebury Clo. SN11 17 A3
Azalea Clo. SN11 17 C5
Back Rd. SN11 17 C4
Baily Ho. SN11 17 C3
Bay Clo. SN11 17 C3
Baydon Gro. SN11 17 B1
Bentley Gro. SN11 17 C4
Beversbrook Rd. SN11 17 B1
Bishop Rd. SN11 17 B2
Blake Ho. SN11 17 C3
Bluebell Gro. SN11 17 C1
Bodinrar Ho. SN11 17 C3
Braemor Rd. SN11 17 A2
Bremhill Vw. SN11 17 A1
Brewers La. SN11 17 C4
Broken Cross. SN11 17 C3
Bryans Close Rd. SN11 17 B2
Campion Clo. SN11 17 B1
Canal Clo. SN11 17 B4
Carnegie Mews. SN11 17 B3
Carnegie Rd. SN11 17 C1
Castle St. SN11 17 B3
Castle Walk. SN11 17 A3
Castlefields. SN11 17 B3
Charlieu Av. SN11 17 C6
Chavey Well Ct. SN11 17 B3
Cherry Tree Ct. SN11 17 B1
Chilvester Hill. SN11 17 A3
Church St. SN11 17 B3
Churchill Clo. SN11 17 C4
Clark Av. SN11 17 C1
Colemans Clo. SN11 17 C3
Cop Clo. SN11 17 B3
Corfe Cres. SN11 17 A2
Cornflower Clo. SN11 17 C1
Coulter Ho. SN11 17 C3
Cowslip Gro. SN11 17 B1
Coxs Hill. SN11 17 B3
Curzon Clo. SN11 17 A3
Curzon St. SN11 17 A3
Dixon Way. SN11 17 B2
Downland Rd. SN11 17 B3
Druids Clo. SN11 17 A3
Duncan St. SN11 17 B1
Dunnet Clo. SN11 17 C2
Ebor Gdns. SN11 17 C6
Ebor Paddock. SN11 17 C6
Elm Clo. SN11 17 C6
Ernle Rd. SN11 17 C2
Fairway. SN11 17 C6
Falcon Rd. SN11 17 D3
Fitz Sq. SN11 17 C3
Foreman St. SN11 17 C3
Foxglove Way. SN11 17 B1
Fynamore Gdns. SN11 17 B4
Fynamore Pl. SN11 17 C2
George Clo. SN11 17 C3
Grierson Clo. SN11 17 C3
Guthrie Rd. SN11 17 C1
Harris Rd. SN11 17 C1
Hazel Gro. SN11 17 B5
Hazell Clo. SN11 17 C1
Heather Way. SN11 17 C5
Heron Clo. SN11 17 D3
High St. SN11 17 B3
Highgrove Clo. SN11 17 D3
Holly Clo. SN11 17 C5
Honey Garston. SN11 17 C2
Honeymead. SN11 17 C2
Horsebrook. SN11 17 C4
Horsebrook Pk. SN11 17 C4
Hungerford Rd. SN11 17 C2

INDUSTRIAL & RETAIL:
Portemarsh Ind Est.
 SN11 17 C1
Station Rd Ind Est.
 SN11 17 B4
Jasmine Clo. SN11 17 C5
Keevil Av. SN11 17 A3
Kerry Cres. SN11 17 B3
Kingsbury St. SN11 17 B3
Lansdowne Clo. SN11 17 A2
Lickhill Rd. SN11 17 B1
Lilac Way. SN11 17 B5
Lime Tree Clo. SN11 17 A3
Linden Clo. SN11 17 B4
*Lodge Clo,
 Longbarrow Rd. SN11 17 A3
London Rd. SN11 17 C4
Longbarrow Rd. SN11 17 A3
Low La. SN11 17 C4
Luckett Way. SN11 17 C1
Macaulay Sq. SN11 17 C3
Magnolia Rise. SN11 17 B5
Mallard Clo. SN11 17 D3
Maple Clo. SN11 17 C5
Marden Way. SN11 17 B4
Market Hill. SN11 17 B3
Martin Way. SN11 17 D3
Maundrell Rd. SN11 17 C1
Meadow Vw. SN11 17 D6
Mill St. SN11 17 B4
Nestleton Clo. SN11 17 B4
New Rd. SN11 17 B3
Newcroft Clo. SN11 17 B1
Newcroft Rd. SN11 17 B1
North End. SN11 17 A2
North St. SN11 17 B2
Northcote. SN11 17 B2
Northway. SN11 17 A2
Ogilvie Sq. SN11 17 C3
Oldbury Prior. SN11 17 C5
Oldbury Way. SN11 17 A3
Orchard Clo. SN11 17 C4
Oxford Rd. SN11 17 B3
Page Clo. SN11 17 C3
Park Clo. SN11 17 D4
Patford St. SN11 17 B3
Penn Hill Rd. SN11 17 C2
Phelps Par. SN11 17 B3
Pinnhills. SN11 17 B4
Pinniger Ho. SN11 17 C3
Porte Marsh Rd. SN11 17 C1
Portland Pl. SN11 17 D4
Portland Way. SN11 17 D4
Priestley Gro. SN11 17 C4
Primrose Clo. SN11 17 B1
Prince Charles Dri.
 SN11 17 C3
Pym Ho. SN11 17 C3
Quarr Barton. SN11 17 B3
Quarry Dale Clo. SN11 17 C4
Ridgemead. SN11 17 B1
Riverside. SN11 17 D6
Rochdale Av. SN11 17 B1
Roundhouse. SN11 17 D5
Saddle Back Clo. SN11 17 B3
St Catherines Clo. SN11 17 C2
St Dunstan Clo. SN11 17 B1
St Margarets Clo. SN11 17 A2
St Nicholas Clo. SN11 17 C2
Sand Pit Rd. SN11 17 D1
Sandy Ridge. SN11 17 C4
Sarum Way. SN11 17 A3
Savernake Dri. SN11 17 A3
Shelburne Rd. SN11 17 C4
Silbury Rd. SN11 17 A3
Silver St. SN11 17 B5
South Pl. SN11 17 B4
Springfield Dri. SN11 17 A2
Station Rd. SN11 17 B4
Stockley La. SN11 17 C6
Stokes Croft. SN11 17 B2
Swaddon St. SN11 17 B2
Tamarisk Clo. SN11 17 C5
Tern Clo. SN11 17 D3
The Glebe. SN11 17 C3
The Green. SN11 17 C4
The Knapp. SN11 17 C3
The Pippin. SN11 17 B3
The Quarry. SN11 17 B5
The Rise. SN11 17 C6
The Slades. SN11 17 C2
The Square. SN11 17 B3
The Strand. SN11 17 B3
The Wharf. SN11 17 B3
The Wynd. SN11 17 B2
Thomas Ct. SN11 17 C4
Trinity Pk. SN11 17 C5
Tyning Pk. SN11 17 C5
Valley View. SN11 17 B4
Vicarage Clo. SN11 17 C3
Victoria Ter. SN11 17 B2
*Walter Sutton Clo,
 Longbarrow Rd. SN11 17 A3
Wansdyke Dri. SN11 17 A3
Warren Cres. SN11 17 C2
Wenhill Heights. SN11 17 B4
Wenhill La. SN11 17 B4
Wessex Clo. SN11 17 D3
Wessington Av. SN11 17 C5
Wessington Clo. SN11 17 C5
Wessington Pk. SN11 17 D5
Westerham Wk. SN11 17 D4
White Horse Way.
 SN11 17 B5
William St. SN11 17 C1
Wood St. SN11 17 B2
Woodhill Av. SN11 17 C2
Woodhill Rise. SN11 17 C2
Woodland Pk. SN11 17 B4
Woodroffe Sq. SN11 17 C3
Wyvern Av. SN11 17 D3
Yew Tree Clo. SN11 17 A3

CHIPPENHAM

Acacia Clo. SN14 18 A2
Allington Way. SN14 18 A2
Andrews Clo. SN14 18 B4
Applewood Clo. SN14 18 C3
Arundel Clo. SN14 18 A4
Ascot Clo. SN14 18 A6
Ashe Cres. SN15 18 D1
Ashfield Rd. SN15 18 D2
Audley Rd. SN14 18 C4
Avebury Rd. SN14 18 A5
Avenue La Fleche.
 SN15 18 D4
Avonmead. SN15 19 F3
Awdry Clo. SN14 18 A4
Bakehouse Clo. SN15 19 E4
Barken Rd. SN14 18 A2
Barn Clo. SN14 18 A3
Barn Owl Clo. SN14 18 B1
Barnes Rd. SN14 18 B1
Barons Mead. SN14 18 A3
Barrow Grn. SN15 19 E1
Bath Rd,
 Hungerdown. SN14 18 A6
Bath Rd,
 Lowden. SN15 18 C5
Baydons La. SN15 19 E5
Bayliffes Clo. SN15 19 G4
Beale Clo. SN14 18 A4
Beechwood Rd. SN14 18 C3
Bellinger Clo. SN15 18 D1
Berkley Clo. SN14 18 A4
Birch Gro. SN15 18 D2
Birds Marsh Vw. SN15 19 E1
Blackberry Clo. SN14 18 A1
Blackbridge Rd. SN15 19 F3
Blackcross. SN15 19 F5
Bluebell Dri. SN14 18 B1
Boothmead. SN14 18 B3
Borough Par. SN15 18 D4
Boundary Rd. SN15 19 F4
Bradbury Clo. SN15 19 G6
Brake Mead. SN15 19 F4
Bright Clo. SN15 19 F6
Brinkworth Clo. SN14 18 A4
Bristol Rd. SN14 18 A1
Brittain Clo. SN14 18 A4
Brook St. SN14 18 B3
Brookwell Clo. SN15 18 C1
Broomfield. SN15 18 D1
Brotherton Clo. SN15 19 F6
Bruges Clo. SN15 19 F4
Brunel Ct. SN14 18 B5
Bulls Hill. SN15 19 E5
Bumpers Farm Way.
 SN14 18 A3
Burlands Rd. SN15 19 E5
Burleaze. SN15 18 C6
Bythebrook. SN14 18 B2
Canterbury St. SN14 18 C3
Carnarvon Clo. SN14 18 A5
Carpenter Clo. SN15 19 F6
Castlehaven Clo. SN15 19 G6
Causeway Clo. SN15 19 E5
Cedar Gro. SN15 19 F2
Celandine Way. SN14 18 B1
Chamberlain Rd. SN14 18 A4
Chapel La. SN15 19 E4
Charter Rd. SN15 18 D4
Cheltenham Dri. SN14 18 A6
Chelwood Clo. SN14 18 B5
Chepstow Clo. SN14 18 A6
Chester Way. SN14 18 A6
Chestnut Rd. SN14 18 C3
Cheval Clo. SN14 18 B1
Church View. SN15 18 C1
Clift Av. SN15 19 E2
Clift Ho. SN15 18 D2
Clifton Clo. SN14 18 B3
Clover Dean. SN14 18 A5
Cockleberry La. SN15 19 E1
Cockleberry Rd. SN15 19 E3
Colborne Clo. SN15 19 H6
College Clo. SN15 19 F3
Collen Clo. SN14 18 A4
Common Slip. SN15 19 E4
Coniston Rd. SN14 18 A5
Conway Rd. SN14 18 A4
Cranwell Clo. SN14 18 A6
Cricketts La. SN15 19 F6
Crown Clo. SN15 19 G6
Culverwell Rd. SN14 18 A4
Curlew Dri. SN14 18 A1
Dallas Rd. SN15 18 C3
Danes Clo. SN15 19 F6
Darcy Clo. SN15 19 F3
Deansway. SN15 18 D1
Deansway Ct. SN15 18 D1
Derby Clo. SN15 19 F6
Derriads Grn. SN14 18 A4
Derriads La. SN14 18 A4
Dover St. SN14 18 C4
Down View. SN14 18 A4
Downham Mead. SN15 18 A4
Downing St. SN14 18 C3
Dummer Way. SN15 19 G6
Dyers Clo. SN15 19 G6
Eastern Av. SN15 19 F3
Easton La. SN14 18 A6
Edridge Clo. SN15 19 F3
Elmwood. SN15 18 D1
Emery La. SN15 19 E4
Erleigh Dri. SN15 19 F3
Esmead. SN15 19 F3
Evans Clo. SN15 19 E2
Fairfoot Clo. SN14 18 A5
Fallow Field Clo. SN14 18 B1
Farleigh Clo. SN14 18 A5
Farmer Clo. SN15 19 E1
Field Vw. SN15 18 D3
Fleet Rd. SN15 18 D4
Fogham Shire. SN15 18 D4
Folkestone Clo. SN14 18 A6
Forest La. SN15 19 F6
Fortune Way. SN15 19 F6
Foundry La. SN15 19 E3
Fox Clo. SN14 18 B1
Foxgrove. SN14 18 A1
Frogwell. SN14 18 A3
Frogwell Pk. SN14 18 A3
Gales Clo. SN15 19 F3
Garrick Clo. SN15 19 G3
Garth Clo. SN14 18 B1
Gascelyn Clo. SN14 18 A4
Gastons Rd. SN14 18 B3
Gipsy La. SN15 18 D5
Gladstone Rd. SN15 18 D4
Gleneagles Clo. SN15 19 F4
Glendale Dri. SN15 19 E5
Gloucester Clo. SN14 18 A5
Goldney Av. SN15 18 C4
Goodwood Way. SN14 18 A6
Greenway Av. SN15 18 D2
Greenway Ct. SN15 18 D1
Greenway Gdns. SN15 18 D2
Greenway La. SN15 18 D1
Greenway Pk . SN15 18 D2
Gundry Clo. SN15 19 F5
Habrels Clo. SN15 19 F5
Hancock Clo. SN15 19 G6
Hardenhuish Av. SN14 18 C3
Hardenhuish La. SN14 18 B2
Hardens Clo. SN15 19 G6
Hardens Mead. SN15 19 G6
Hares Patch. SN14 18 B1
Harford Clo. SN15 19 F6
Harnish Way. SN15 18 B1
Hawkins Clo. SN15 19 F6
Hawthorn Rd. SN15 19 E2
Haydock Clo. SN14 18 A6
Heathfield. SN15 19 E1
Hereford Clo. SN14 18 A6
Hewlett Clo. SN15 19 F6
High St. SN15 19 E4
Hill Corner Rd. SN15 18 D1
Hill Rise. SN15 19 E1
Hither Clo. SN14 18 A3
Hollybush Clo. SN14 18 A1
Honeybrook Clo. SN14 18 B3
Hungerdown La. SN14 18 A6
Hungerford Rd. SN15 18 D2

INDUSTRIAL & RETAIL:
Bath Rd Ind Est. SN14 18 B5
Bumpus Farm
 Ind Est. SN14 18 A2
Greenways Business
 Park. SN15 18 D1
Herman Miller
 Ind Est. SN14 18 B6
Lansdowne Ct
 Business Park. SN14 18 A3
Parsonage Way
 Ind Est. SN15 19 F1
Ivy La. SN15 18 D4
Ivy Rd. SN15 18 D4
Ivyfield Ct. SN15 18 D4
Jasmine Clo. SN14 18 A3
Jordan Clo. SN15 19 F6
Kelso Ct. SN14 18 A6
Kent Clo. SN14 18 A5
Kilverts Clo. SN14 18 A5
King Alfred St. SN14 18 C3
Kingham Clo. SN15 18 C4
Kingsley Rd. SN14 18 B5
Lackham Circus. SN15 18 B5
Ladds La. SN15 19 E5
Lady Coventry Rd.
 SN15 19 F4

Ladyfield Rd. SN14 18 B5
Laines Head. SN15 18 C1
Lamberts. SN14 18 B3
Langley Rd. SN15 19 E2
Lanhill Vw. SN14 18 B1
Lansdown Gro. SN15 19 E2
Lapwing Cres. SN15 18 B1
Laurel Dri. SN15 18 C5
Lenton Clo. SN14 18 A4
Little Down. SN14 18 B4
Little Englands. SN15 19 E5
Littlecote Rd. SN14 18 A5
Lockside. SN15 19 F6
Lodge Rd. SN15 19 G6
London Rd. SN15 19 E5
Long Clo. SN15 19 F5
Long Ridings. SN15 18 C1
Longstone. SN14 18 A2
Lords Mead. SN14 18 A3
Lovers Walk. SN15 18 C5
Lowden. SN15 18 C5
Lowden Av. SN15 18 C3
Lowden Hill. SN15 18 C4
Loyalty St. SN14 18 C4
Ludlow Clo. SN15 19 G6
Lydiard Rd. SN14 18 A5
Lytham Clo. SN15 19 F4
Malmesbury Rd. SN15 18 C1
Manor Rd. SN14 18 A3
Maple Way. SN15 18 D1
Market Pl. SN15 19 E4
Marlborough Ct. SN14 18 C4
Marshall St. SN14 18 C4
Marshfield Rd. SN14 18 C3
Martins Clo. SN15 19 G3
Matford Hill. SN15 19 G3
Maud Heaths Causeway. SN15 19 E1
Maur Clo. SN15 18 A4
Meadow Clo. SN14 18 A4
Melksham Way. SN15 18 B6
Milestone Way. SN15 18 D1
Minster Way. SN14 18 A6
Monkton Clo. SN14 18 D4
Montague Clo. SN15 19 G4
Moorlands. SN15 19 E1
Mulberry Clo. SN14 18 B2
Murrayfield. SN15 19 E2
Neeld Cres. SN14 18 B3
New La. SN15 18 D3
New Rd. SN15 18 D3
Newall Tuck Rd. SN4 19 F4
Newbury Dri. SN14 18 A6
Northwood. SN15 19 E1
Oak Lodge Clo. SN15 18 C3
Oaklands. SN15 18 D1
Oate Hill. SN15 19 F5
Odcroft Clo. SN15 19 F4
O'Donnell Clo. SN15 19 E1
Old Hardenhuish La. SN14 18 B2
Old Rd. SN15 18 D3
Orchard Cres. SN14 18 B4
Orchard Rd. SN14 18 B4
Page Clo. SN14 18 A4
Palmer St. SN14 18 C4
Park Av. SN14 18 B3
Park La. SN14 18 D3
Park Ter. SN14 18 C3
Parkfields. SN14 18 C3
Parkside. SN15 18 D3
Parliament St. SN14 18 B4
Parsonage Way. SN15 19 F1
Partridge Clo. SN15 18 B1
Patchway. SN14 18 B3
Pavely Clo. SN15 18 C5
Pew Hill. SN15 19 E1
Pewsham Lock. SN15 19 E6
Pewsham Way. SN15 19 E6
Pewsham Way. SN15 19 H6
Picketleaze. SN14 18 A4
Pipsmore Rd. SN14 18 A3
Plantation. SN14 18 C3
Popham Ct. SN15 19 E5
Portway. SN14 18 B5
Primrose Way. SN14 18 B1
Queens Cres. SN14 18 A5
Queens Sq. SN15 19 E5
Ray Clo. SN15 19 F6
Redland. SN14 18 B3
Redwing Av. SN15 18 B1
Ricardo Rd. SN15 18 C1
Ridings Mead. SN15 18 C1
Ripon Clo. SN14 18 A6
River St. SN15 19 E4
Riverside Dri. SN15 19 G4

Robins Clo. SN15 18 B1
Roman Way. SN15 19 G6
Rowden Hill. SN15 18 C5
Rowden La. SN15 18 C6
Rowden Rd. SN15 18 C6
Rowe Mead. SN15 19 E6
Royal Clo. SN15 18 B1
Rumble Dene. SN15 19 E6
Ryan Av. SN14 18 A4
Sadlers Mead. SN15 19 E3
St Clements Clo. SN14 18 C3
St Francis Av. SN15 18 C5
St Josephs Dri. SN15 18 C5
St Lukes Clo. SN15 18 C5
St Margarets Gdns. SN15 18 C5
St Mary St. SN15 19 E4
St Marys Pl. SN15 18 D3
St Mellion Clo. SN15 19 F2
St Paul St. SN15 18 D3
St Peters Clo. SN15 18 C5
St Teresa's Dri. SN15 18 C5
Salisbury Clo. SN14 18 A5
Saltersford La. SN15 18 A6
Sandes Clo. SN15 18 C4
Sandown Dri. SN14 18 A6
Sandpiper Gdns. SN14 18 A1
Sarum Rd. SN14 18 A5
Saxby Rd. SN15 19 E1
Saxon St. SN14 18 B3
School Walk. SN14 18 A4
Selions Clo. SN14 18 B1
Seymour Rd. SN15 19 F3
Sheepscroft. SN14 18 B1
Sheldon Rd. SN15 18 B4
Silbury Clo. SN14 18 A6
Sorrel Clo. SN14 18 B1
Southmead. SN14 18 B5
Southwell Clo. SN14 18 A6
Spanbourn Av. SN15 18 D4
Spinney Clo. SN14 18 A5
Springfields Bldgs. SN15 18 D3
Stainers Way. SN14 18 A1
Station Hill. SN15 18 D3
Stockwood Rd. SN14 18 B5
Stonelea. SN14 18 B4
Sunningdale Clo. SN15 19 F4
Sydney Wood Ct. SN14 18 C4
Tall Trees. SN15 18 D4
The Battens. SN14 18 A2
The Bridge. SN14 18 D4
The Butts. SN15 19 E5
The Causeway. SN15 19 E4
The Cloisters. SN15 18 D5
The Firs. SN14 18 A5
The Hamlet. SN14 18 D2
The Oaks. SN15 18 D1
The Paddocks. SN15 19 E5
The Poplars. SN14 18 A2
The Tinings. SN15 19 F3
Thirsk Clo. SN14 18 A6
Timber St. SN15 18 D3
Timbrells Pl. SN15 18 C5
Torr Clo. SN14 18 B1
Truro Walk. SN14 18 A5
Tugela Rd. SN15 19 E2
Turnberry Clo. SN15 19 F4
Turpin Way. SN14 18 A4
Twickenham Way. SN15 19 E2
Union Rd. SN15 18 D3
Unity St. SN14 18 C4
Upper Farm Barns. SN14 18 B1
Utterson View. SN15 18 C4
Villiers Clo. SN15 19 F4
Vincients Rd. SN14 18 A2
Wardour Rd. SN14 18 A5
Waters Edge. SN15 19 E6
Weavern Ct. SN14 18 A4
Webb Clo. SN15 19 E6
Webbington Rd. SN15 19 E6
Wedmore Av. SN15 18 D2
Wells Clo. SN14 18 A6
Wentworth Clo. SN15 19 F4
Wessex Rd. SN14 18 B3
West Cepen Way. SN4 18 A1
Westbrook Clo. SN15 18 A4
Westcroft. SN14 18 B6
Westerleigh Clo. SN14 18 B5
Westmead La. SN15 18 D5
Westmead Ter. SN15 19 E5
Westminster Gdns. SN14 18 B4
Wetherby Clo. SN14 18 A6

Whittle Clo. SN14 18 A4
Wicks Dri. SN15 19 F6
Willow Gro. SN15 19 E1
Willowbank. SN14 18 B2
Winchester Clo. SN14 18 A5
Windlass Way. SN15 19 F6
Windsor Clo. SN14 18 A5
Wishart Way. SN15 19 F6
Wood La. SN15 19 F6
Woodlands Rd. SN14 18 C4
Woodpecker Clo. SN14 18 B1
Wyndham Clo. SN15 19 F3
Yewstock Cres East. SN15 18 C2
Yewstock Cres West. SN15 18 C2
York Clo. SN14 18 A5

CORSHAM

Academy Dri. SN13 20 C2
Alexander Ter. SN13 20 D2
Allen Rd. SN13 20 A3
Arney Clo. SN13 20 C3
Arnolds Mead. SN13 20 D2
Barn Clo. SN13 20 C3
Basil Hill Rd. SN13 20 A4
Bath Rd. SN13 20 A2
Beechfield Rd. SN13 20 C2
Bellott Dri. SN13 20 C2
Bences La. SN13 20 E1
Bethel Rd. SN13 20 A3
Bradford Rd. SN13 20 A3
Brakspear Dri. SN13 20 F4
Broadmead. SN13 20 F4
Brook Dri. SN13 20 D2
Brunel Clo. SN13 20 D2
Burn Rd. SN13 20 C2
Charles St. SN13 20 D2
Charlwood Rd. SN13 20 C3
Chestnut Grange. SN13 20 B2
Church St. SN13 20 E2
Churchill Way. SN13 20 D1
Clevedale Rd. SN13 20 E4
Coulston Rd. SN13 20 E1
Cresswells. SN13 20 D3
Cross Keys Rd. SN13 20 C2
Curl Croft Rd. SN13 20 B4
Danvers Rd. SN13 20 C2
Dew Clo. SN13 20 C2
Dickens Av. SN13 20 C2
Dicketts Rd. SN13 20 C2
Dovecote Dri. SN13 20 C2
Edridge Pl. SN13 20 C3
Elm Gro. SN13 20 C2
Elm Hayes. SN13 20 E4
Erneston Vw. SN13 20 D2
Etherhed Pl. SN13 20 C2
Fuller Av. SN13 20 C3
Furzehill. SN13 20 D3
Glebe Way. SN13 20 D3
Grove Rd. SN13 20 E3
Hardhams Rise. SN13 20 D4
Hartham La. SN13 20 D1
Hastings Rd. SN13 20 E3
Hatton Way. SN13 20 C3
High St. SN13 20 E2
Hitherspring. SN13 20 D4
Hudswell La. SN13 20 A4
Hulbert Clo. SN13 20 C3
INDUSTRIAL & RETAIL:
Park La Ind Est. SN13 20 A3
Ivy Field. SN13 20 E2
Jargeau Ct. SN13 20 E3
Kings Av. SN13 20 D1
Kirby Rd. SN13 20 C2
Lacock Rd. SN13 20 E4
Ladbrook La. SN13 20 F4
Light Clo. SN13 20 E4
Ludmead Rd. SN13 20 E4
Lypiatt Mead. SN13 20 E4
Lypiatt Rd. SN13 20 E4
Manor Rd. SN13 20 D1
Masons Way. SN13 20 E4
Mayo Clo. SN13 20 C2
Meadland. SN13 20 C2
Meriton Av. SN13 20 C2
Methuen Way. SN13 20 D1
Middlewick La. SN13 20 C1
Neale Clo. SN13 20 E4
Newlands Rd. SN13 20 E2
Nursery Gdns. SN13 20 E2
Oathills. SN13 20 D3
Oliver Av. SN13 20 D2

Orchard Rd. SN13 20 D1
Paddock La. SN13 20 B3
Park La. SN13 20 A4
Partridge Clo. SN13 20 C3
Paul St. SN13 20 D3
Peel Circus. SN13 20 E3
Penleigh Clo. SN13 20 D3
Pickwick Rd. SN13 20 C2
Pictor Clo. SN13 20 B3
Pockeredge Dri. SN13 20 A4
Pockeredge Rd. SN13 20 A4
Post Office La. SN13 20 E2
Potley La. SN13 20 C3
Pound Hill Prospect. SN13 20 E3
Pound Mead. SN13 20 D4
Poynder Rd. SN13 20 D3
Priory New Rd. SN13 20 D2
Priory St. SN13 20 D2
Providence Rd. SN13 20 D2
Purleigh Rd. SN13 20 C2
Queens Av. SN13 20 D1
Randall Ct. SN13 20 B2
St Barbaras Rd. SN13 20 B3
Saunders Gro. SN13 20 B3
Savernake Rd. SN13 20 B4
Shearwater Way. SN13 20 B4
Sheffield La. SN13 20 B3
Silman Clo. SN13 20 B2
Smiths Yd. SN13 20 E2
South St. SN13 20 E3
Southerwicks. SN13 20 D3
Spackman La. SN13 20 E2
Spring Gdns. SN13 20 E2
Spring La. SN13 20 A4
Station Rd. SN13 20 E3
Stokes Rd. SN13 20 E3
Sumsions Dri. SN13 20 B3
Swan Rd. SN13 20 C3
Syon Clo. SN13 20 C3
Tacker Clo. SN13 20 C3
Tellcroft Clo. SN13 20 D4
The Cleeve. SN13 20 E4
The Knowle. SN13 20 E4
The Laggar. SN13 20 D1
The Precinct. SN13 20 E2
The Tynings. SN13 20 E3
Tropenell Clo. SN13 20 C3
Tupman Rd. SN13 20 C2
Upper Potley. SN13 20 B4
Valley Rd. SN13 20 D2
Weller Rd. SN13 20 C2
West Park Rd. SN13 20 C2
Williams Gro. SN13 20 E3
Woodborough Rd. SN13 20 F4
Woodlands. SN13 20 C2
Yockney Clo. SN13 20 D2
York Clo. SN13 20 D1

CRICKLADE

Abingdon Ct La. SN6 21 C5
Bailiffs Piece. SN6 21 B4
Bath Ct. SN6 21 B5
Bath Rd. SN6 21 A5
Bishopsfields. SN6 21 A5
Branders. SN6 21 B4
Calcutt St. SN6 21 C5
Chelworth Rd. SN6 21 A6
Cherrytree Rd. SN6 21 B5
Church La. SN6 21 C4
Cirencester Rd. SN6 21 C4
Cliffords. SN6 21 A5
Common Hill. SN6 21 A5
Cricklade By-Pass. SN6 21 C4
Deansfield. SN6 21 A6
Doubledays. SN6 21 B5
Fairfield. SN6 21 B4
Fairview. SN6 21 C5
Fiddle Farm. SN6 21 B4
Foxleaze. SN6 21 B4
Fullers Av. SN6 21 B5
Galley Orchard. SN6 21 C5
Gas La. SN6 21 B5
Giles Av. SN6 21 B6
Hallsfield. SN6 21 C5
Hammonds. SN6 21 C5
High St. SN6 21 B5
Homeground. SN6 21 A4
Hopkins Orchard. SN6 21 B6
Horse Fair La. SN6 21 B4
Kitefield. SN6 21 B4
Lady Mead. SN6 21 A5

Malmesbury Rd. SN6 21 A5
Manor Orchard. SN6 21 C5
Middle Ground. SN6 21 A4
North Keels. SN6 21 A4
North Meadow Rd. SN6 21 A4
North Wall. SN6 21 B4
Ockwells. SN6 21 B6
Parsonage Farm La. SN6 21 B5
Pauls Croft. SN6 21 B6
Pike House Clo. SN6 21 A5
Pittsfield. SN6 21 B6
Pleydells. SN6 21 B4
Purton Rd. SN6 21 B6
Rectory La. SN6 21 C4
Red Lion La. SN6 21 C4
Reeds. SN6 21 A4
Saxon Clo. SN6 21 B5
Spital La. SN6 21 C5
Stones La. SN6 21 A5
Swindon Rd. SN6 21 C5
Thames Clo. SN6 21 C5
Thames La. SN6 21 C5
The Fiddle. SN6 21 A5
The Forty. SN6 21 B6
Water Furlong. SN6 21 B6
Waylands. SN6 21 B6
West Mill La. SN6 21 A4
White Horse Rd. SN6 21 B5

DEVIZES

Addington Clo. SN10 23 F5
Anstie Clo. SN10 23 G3
Ash Walk. SN10 23 H1
Avon Clo. SN10 22 B4
Avon Ter. SN10 23 E3
Badgers Clo. SN10 23 F5
Bath Rd. SN10 22 A4
Beau Clerc St. SN10 22 C4
Beechfield Dri. SN10 23 H2
Beechwood Dri. SN10 23 H1
Belle Vue Rd. SN10 22 D3
Bratton Av. SN10 23 G5
Brickham Rd. SN10 23 G3
Brickley La. SN10 23 G3
Bricksteed Av. SN10 23 G4
Bridewell St. SN10 23 F4
Broadleas Clo. SN10 23 E5
Broadleas Cres. SN10 23 E6
Broadleas Pk. SN10 23 E6
Broadleas Rd. SN10 23 E5
Byron Rd. SN10 23 F6
Caen Hill Gdns. SN10 22 B4
Caird Lawns. SN10 23 G5
Canal Way. SN10 23 H2
Castle Ct. SN10 23 E4
Castle La. SN10 23 E4
Castle Rd. SN10 23 E4
Chandler Clo. SN10 23 G4
Chantry Ct. SN10 23 F3
Charles Morrison Clo. SN10 23 E4
Charter Clo. SN10 23 G2
Church Walk. SN10 23 E4
Church Yard. SN10 23 E4
Coate La. SN10 23 H2
Colston Rd. SN10 23 E3
Commercial Rd. SN10 23 E3
Consciences La. SN10 22 B1
Coping Clo. SN10 23 F4
Cornfield Rd. SN10 23 E4
Cornwall Cres. SN10 23 E5
Couch La. SN10 23 E3
Cowslip Clo. SN10 23 H2
Cranesbill Rd. SN10 23 H2
Cromwell Rd. SN10 23 G4
Cunnington Clo. SN10 23 G3
Cygnet Clo. SN10 23 H2
Devizes Rd. SN10 22 A1
Downlands Rd. SN10 23 F6
Drakes Av. SN10 23 F5
Drews Pond La. SN10 23 F6
Dundas Clo. SN10 22 B4
Dunkirk Hill. SN10 22 C3
Dyehouse La. SN10 23 E2
Eastleigh Clo. SN10 23 G5
Eastleigh Rd. SN10 23 G5
Edward Rd. SN10 23 F5
Elcombe Gdns. SN10 23 E3
Elizabeth Dri. SN10 23 G3
Elliott Ct. SN10 23 F6
Elmtree Clo. SN10 23 H5

Elmtree Gdns. SN10 23 H5
Estcourt Cres. SN10 23 F3
Estcourt Hill. SN10 23 E4
Estcourt St. SN10 23 F3
Ferguson Rd. SN10 23 G6
Fordson Rd. SN10 23 G6
Forty Acres Rd. SN10 23 G4
Furlong Clo. SN10 22 A2
Furze Hill. SN10 22 C6
Gables Clo. SN10 23 G5
Gains La. SN10 23 F3
Granary Clo. SN10 23 G4
Granary Rd. SN10 23 G4
Great Western Clo. SN10 23 E3
Green La. SN10 23 F6
Greenfield Rd. SN10 23 G6
Gundry Clo. SN10 23 G3
Hambleton Av. SN10 23 H1
Hare & Hounds St. SN10 23 F4
Harebell Way. SN10 23 H2
Hartfield. SN10 23 E5
Hartmoor Rd. SN10 22 D6
High Lawn. SN10 22 C3
High St, Devizes. SN10 23 F4
High St, Rowde. SN10 22 A1
Hill Rd. SN10 23 G6
Hillworth Gdns. SN10 23 E4
Hillworth Rd. SN10 22 E4
Hodge Clo. SN10 23 H4
Hopkins Clo. SN10 23 H4
Hopton Rd. SN10 23 H1
INDUSTRIAL & RETAIL:
Garden Trading Est. SN10 23 G2
Hopton Ind Est. SN10 23 H1
Nursteed Ind Est. SN10 23 G5
Jackson Clo. SN10 23 G5
John Rennie Clo. SN10 22 D5
John Rumble Ct. SN10 23 F4
Jump Farm Rd. SN10 23 G3
Kemp Clo. SN10 23 G3
Kempsfield. SN10 23 G6
Kennet Rd. SN10 23 G5
Kingfisher Dri. SN10 23 H1
Kingsley Gdns. SN10 23 G4
Kingsley Rd. SN10 23 G4
Kingsmanor Wharf. SN10 23 H2
Kirby Clo. SN10 23 G3
*Lansdowne Gro, Sheep St. SN10 23 F4
*Lansdowne Ter, Sheep St. SN10 23 F4
Lawrence Clo. SN10 23 F6
Le Marchant Clo. SN10 23 H2
Lewis's Ct. SN10 23 E3
Linden Ter. SN10 23 F4
Little Brittox. SN10 23 E3
London Rd. SN10 23 G3
Long St. SN10 23 E4
Longcroft Av. SN10 23 G4
Longcroft Cres. SN10 23 G4
Longcroft Rd. SN10 23 G4
Longfields Walk. SN10 23 G5
Lower Wharf. SN10 23 E3
Market Pl. SN10 23 E3
Marsh La. SN10 22 A1
Marshall Rd. SN10 23 F4
Maryport St. SN10 23 F4
Maslen Clo. SN10 23 H4
Massey Rd. SN10 23 G6
Matilda Way. SN10 23 G2
Mattock Clo. SN10 23 G3
Maud Clo. SN10 23 G2
Maundrell Clo. SN10 22 A1
Mayenne Pl. SN10 22 B4
Meadow Dri. SN10 23 F4
Meads Pl. SN10 23 F4
Middle Field Clo. SN10 23 G4
Mill Clo. SN10 23 G6
Monday Market St. SN10 23 F3
Moonrakers. SN10 23 H2
Morris La. SN10 22 D3
Moyne Clo. SN10 22 D3
Neate Rd. SN10 23 G3
New Park Rd. SN10 23 E3
New Park St. SN10 23 E3
Northgate Gdns. SN10 23 E3
Northgate St. SN10 23 E3
Nursteed Clo. SN10 23 H5
Nursteed Pk. SN10 23 G5
Nursteed Rd. SN10 23 F4
Oamaru Way. SN10 23 G4

Offers Ct. SN10 23 F4
Orchard Clo. SN10 23 F6
Pans La. SN10 23 F4
Park Vw. SN10 22 C4
Parkfields. SN10 23 G2
Phillip Clo. SN10 23 G3
Pines Rd. SN10 23 G4
Potterne Rd. SN10 23 E6
Prince Maurice Ct. SN10 23 H1
Proudman Rd. SN10 23 H3
Quakers Walk. SN10 23 F3
Quarry Clo. SN10 23 G4
Queens Rd. SN10 23 E5
Radnor Clo. SN10 23 F5
Redhorn Gdns. SN10 23 F5
Reed Clo. SN10 23 H4
Reeves Rd. SN10 23 G6
Rendells Ct. SN10 23 F4
Roseland Av. SN10 23 G4
Rotherstone. SN10 23 E3
Roundway Gdns. SN10 23 F1
Roundway Pk. SN10 23 F1
Roundway Rd. SN10 23 H1
Rowde Court Rd. SN10 22 A1
Royal Oak Ct. SN10 23 E3
St Bridget Clo. SN10 23 H4
*St Johns Ct Church Yd. SN10 23 E4
St Johns St. SN10 23 E4
St Josephs Rd. SN10 22 D3
Salisbury St. SN10 22 C4
Sarum Dri. SN10 23 F5
Sedgefield Gdns. SN10 23 F3
Shackleton Rd. SN10 23 H5
Sheep St. SN10 23 F4
Sheppard Clo. SN10 23 E3
Sidmouth St. SN10 23 F4
Snuff St. SN10 23 E3
Southbroom Rd. SN10 23 F4
Southgate. SN10 23 F5
Southgate Clo. SN10 23 F5
Springers Clo. SN10 23 G3
Springfield Rd. SN10 22 A1
Stanley Ter. SN10 23 F5
Station Rd. SN10 22 E3
Steele Clo. SN10 23 G3
Stockwell Rd. SN10 23 G3
Sussex Wharf. SN10 22 D3
Sutton Pl. SN10 23 F4
Tanis. SN10 22 B1
The Ark. SN10 23 E4
The Breach. SN10 23 F5
The Brittox. SN10 23 E4
The Croft. SN10 23 G3
The Fairway. SN10 23 E6
The Moorlands. SN10 23 E5
The Nursery. SN10 22 D3
The Patchway. SN10 23 H4
The Sidings. SN10 22 D4
Thomas Wyatt Rd. SN10 23 F6
Tilley Clo. SN10 23 G4
Tintern Rd. SN10 23 F6
Tornio Clo. SN10 23 H2
Victoria Rd. SN10 23 F3
Waiblingen Way. SN10 22 D3
Walden Lodge Clo. SN10 23 G4
Waylands. SN10 23 G4
Wessex Clo. SN10 23 G4
Westridge. SN10 23 E3
West View Cres. SN10 22 D4
Wharf St. SN10 23 E3
Whistley Rd. SN10 22 A4
Wick La. SN10 23 E5
Wickfield. SN10 23 F5
William Rd. SN10 23 G5
Willow Dri. SN10 23 H2
Windsor Dri. SN10 23 G3
Wine St. SN10 23 E4
Woodland Way. SN10 23 E6

DOWNTON & REDLYNCH

Apple Tree Clo. SP5 25 F3
Appletree Rd. SP5 25 F3
Avon Meadow. SP5 24 C3
Avondyke. SP5 25 B4
Barford La. SP5 24 C2
Barnaby Clo. SP5 24 A3
Batten Rd. SP5 24 A2
Bennett Clo. SP5 25 F4
Besomers Drove. SP5 25 H6

Bowers Hill. SP5 25 G3
Breamore Rd. SP5 24 A5
Castle Meadows. SP5 24 C3
Castle Woods. SP5 25 F4
Catherine Cres. SP5 24 A3
Chalks Clo. SP5 25 F3
Chapel Rd. SP5 25 G4
Church Hatch. SP5 24 C3
Church Hill. SP5 25 H4
Cranbury Clo. SP5 24 C4
Crossways Clo. SP5 24 A3
Dairy Clo. SP5 25 F5
Downlands Clo. SP5 24 C4
Downton Hill. SP5 25 F3
Eastmans Clo. SP5 24 C4
Elizabeth Clo. SP5 24 A3
Elmfield Clo. SP5 25 F5
Forders Clo. SP5 25 F5
Forest Rd. SP5 25 F6
Goggs La. SP5 25 H4
Gravel Clo. SP5 24 B2
Green La. SP5 24 B3
Greenacres. SP5 25 F4
Greens Meade. SP5 25 F4
Grove La. SP5 25 G3
Hamilton Park. SP5 24 C2
Harthill Drove. SP5 25 G4
Herbert Rd. SP5 25 F4
High St. SP5 24 C3
Highfield La. SP5 24 A3
Hyde La. SP5 24 A3
INDUSTRIAL & RETAIL:
Batten Rd Ind Est. SP5 24 A2
Joanna Clo. SP5 24 A3
Kiln Rd. SP5 25 G3
Kingford Clo. SP5 25 F5
Langford La. SP5 25 F3
Little Woodfalls Dri. SP5 25 H6
Lode Hill. SP5 24 D2
Lodge Drove. SP5 25 F6
Long Clo. SP5 24 A2
Loosehanger. SP5 25 H6
Marie Av. SP5 24 A3
Mesh Pond. SP5 24 A3
Mitchells Clo. SP5 25 F4
Moot Clo. SP5 24 C4
Moot Gdns. SP5 24 B4
Moot La. SP5 24 C3
Morgans Rise Rd. SP5 25 F3
Morgans Vale Rd. SP5 25 F3
Muddyford La. SP5 25 G3
Orchard Rd. SP5 25 F4
Petticoat La. SP5 25 G3
Pine View La. SP5 25 F6
Primrose La. SP5 25 E4
Princes Clo. SP5 25 G4
Princes Hill. SP5 25 G3
Quavey Rd. SP5 25 G4
Roman Meadow. SP5 24 C4
Rosedene. SP5 25 G4
St Birinus Rd. SP5 25 F4
St Marys Clo. SP5 25 H6
Salisbury Rd. SP5 24 A1
Sandy La. SP5 25 G2
Saxon Hurst. SP5 24 C3
Saxon Meadow. SP5 24 C3
School Rd. SP5 25 H6
Slab La. SP5 24 D3
Snail Creep. SP5 24 C2
South La. SP5 24 B3
Springfield Cres. SP5 25 F5
Squarey Clo. SP5 24 C4
The Borough. SP5 24 A2
The Close. SP5 25 F3
The Drove. SP5 25 F5
The Headlands. SP5 24 A3
The Ridge. SP5 25 F6
The Row. SP5 25 F3
The Sidings. SP5 24 D2
Tinneys Clo. SP5 24 C4
Twynham Clo. SP5 24 C4
Vale Rd. SP5 25 F4
Valley Clo. SP5 25 F4
Vicarage Pk. SP5 25 F4
Waterside. SP5 24 C3
Wheelwright Mews. SP5 24 A3
Whiteshoot. SP5 25 H6
Whiteshoot Hill. SP5 25 F6
Wick La. SP5 24 A2

HIGHWORTH

Arran Way. SN6 26 A2

Barra Clo. SN6 26 A3
Beech Gro. SN6 26 B4
Biddel Springs. SN6 26 C4
Blandford Alley. SN6 26 B4
Botany. SN6 26 A4
Brewery St. SN6 26 B4
Brookfield. SN6 26 B2
Bute Clo. SN6 26 B2
Byde Mill Gdns. SN6 26 A4
Cherry Orchard. SN6 26 C3
Church Vw. SN6 26 B4
Crane Furlong. SN6 26 B2
Cricklade Rd. SN6 26 A4
Downs View. SN6 26 C3
Eastrop. SN6 26 C4
Edencroft. SN6 26 C2
Folly Clo. SN6 26 B2
Folly Cres. SN6 26 B2
Folly Dri. SN6 26 B2
Folly Way. SN6 26 C2
Grange Clo. SN6 26 C4
Grove Hill. SN6 26 B2
Grove Orchard. SN6 26 B2
Henley Dri. SN6 26 B2
High St. SN6 26 B4
Home Farm. SN6 26 A3
INDUSTRIAL & RETAIL:
Blackworth Ind Est. SN6 26 B1
Islay Cres. SN6 26 B3
Kilda Rd. SN6 26 A2
Kings Av. SN6 26 C4
Knowlands. SN6 26 C2
Lechlade Rd. SN6 26 B4
Lismore Rd. SN6 26 A3
Market Pl. SN6 26 C4
Middi Haines Ct. SN6 26 C3
Newburgh Pl. SN6 26 B3
North Vw. SN6 26 B4
Oak Dri. SN6 26 B4
Orange Clo. SN6 26 B4
Park Av. SN6 26 C4
Parsonage Ct. SN6 26 C4
Pentylands Clo. SN6 26 B2
Pentylands La. SN6 26 B1
Pound Rd. SN6 26 B2
Priory Grn. SN6 26 C3
Quarry Cres. SN6 26 B3
Queens Av. SN6 26 C2
Rivers Pl. SN6 26 B3
Roman Way. SN6 26 A4
Round Hills Mead. SN6 26 C1
St Michaels Clo. SN6 26 A3
Sevenfields. SN6 26 C2
Sheep St. SN6 26 C4
Shrivenham Rd. SN6 26 C5
Skye Clo. SN6 26 A2
Spa Clo. SN6 26 C3
Stapleton Clo. SN6 26 B4
Station Rd. SN6 26 B3
Stonefield Dri. SN6 26 B5
Stranks Clo. SN6 26 C5
Stroma Way. SN6 26 A2
Swindon Rd. SN6 26 B6
Swindon St. SN6 26 B4
The Archers. SN6 26 B3
The Cullerns. SN6 26 C3
The Dormers. SN6 26 C4
The Elms. SN6 26 B4
The Green. SN6 26 B4
The Mews. SN6 26 C4
The Paddocks. SN6 26 C4
The Willows. SN6 26 C4
Turnpike Rd. SN6 26 C3
Vicarage La. SN6 26 B3
Vorda Rd. SN6 26 C2
Wessex Way. SN6 26 D2
Westhill Clo. SN6 26 B4
Westrop. SN6 26 B3
Windrush. SN6 26 A3
Wrde Hill. SN6 26 A4

HOLT

Avonfield. BA14 21 D6
Beales Barton. BA14 21 C5
Beckerley La. BA14 21 C4
Bradford La. BA14 21 A6
Bradley Clo. BA14 21 D5
Bradley La. BA14 21 C5
Chestnut Corner. BA14 21 D5
Crandon Lea. BA14 21 D5
Gipsy La. BA14 21 D4
Great Parks. BA14 21 D4
Green Clo. BA14 21 D6

Ground Corner. BA14 21 B5
Ham Clo. BA14 21 B6
Ham Grn. BA14 21 B6
Hawcroft. BA14 21 C5
INDUSTRIAL & RETAIL:
The Midlands Light Ind Est. BA14 21 C5
Leigh Rd. BA14 21 A4
Little Parks. BA14 21 D4
Maulton Clo. BA14 21 B6
Melksham Rd. BA14 21 D4
Station Rd. BA14 21 C5
Staverton Rd. BA14 21 B6
Stillman Clo. BA14 21 C5
The Common. BA14 21 C5
The Elms. BA14 21 C5
The Gravel. BA14 21 C5
The Midlands. BA14 21 C5
The Star. BA14 21 C6
The Street. BA14 21 C5
The Walk. BA14 21 B6
Three Lions Mws. BA14 21 C5
Woodmand. BA14 21 D6

LUDGERSHALL

Abbatt Clo. SP11 27 F3
Andover Rd. SP11 27 C2
Astor Cres. SP11 27 C3
Bell St. SP11 27 E3
Biddesden La. SP11 27 F3
Brydges Rd. SP11 27 C3
Butt Clo. SP11 27 C2
Byron Clo. SP11 27 C2
Camomile Dri. SP11 27 D3
Castle Cr. SP11 27 C2
Castle St. SP11 27 C2
Central St. SP11 27 D2
Challis Clo. SP11 27 E3
Chapel La. SP11 27 C2
Clarence Gdns. SP11 27 C3
Clover Gdns. SP11 27 D3
Collis Ter. SP11 27 D2
Cornflower Way. SP11 27 D3
Coronation Rd. SP11 27 E3
Crawlboys Rd. SP11 27 D2
Crown La. SP11 27 C2
Deweys La. SP11 27 C2
Edelweiss Clo. SP11 27 D3
Eleanor Ct. SP11 27 C2
Elm Clo. SP11 27 E3
Empress Way. SP11 27 C3
Fleming Clo. SP11 27 D2
Foxtail Gdns. SP11 27 D3
Gould Clo. SP11 27 C2
Graspan Rd. SP11 27 F3
Hei-Lin Way. SP11 27 C2
High St. SP11 27 E3
Hyson Cres. SP11 27 E3
Lady Diana Ct. SP11 27 D2
Lady Jane Wk. SP11 27 D3
Larkin Clo. SP11 27 D3
Laurence Ct. SP11 27 C3
Lena Clo. SP11 27 C3
Levell Ct. SP11 27 C3
Linden Clo. SP11 27 E2
Maple Cres. SP11 27 E3
Meade Rd. SP11 27 E3
New Cres. SP11 27 D3
New Dri. SP11 27 C4
Old Common Way. SP11 27 D2
Orchid Dri. SP11 27 D3
Perham Cres. SP11 27 D2
Pretoria Rd. SP11 27 F3
Primrose Rd. SP11 27 D3
Prince Charles Clo. SP11 27 D2
Princess Mary Gdns. SP11 27 C3
Queens Clo. SP11 27 C3
Recreation Rd. SP11 27 D2
Roberts Rd. SP11 27 C3
Rockrose Ct. SP11 27 C3
St James St. SP11 27 C2
St Nicholas Clo. SP11 27 F3
Shoddesden La. SP11 27 E4
Short St. SP11 27 D2
Simonds Rd. SP11 27 B3
Somme Rd. SP11 27 A3
Spray Leaze. SP11 27 F3
Station App. SP11 27 C2
Stoney Cross. SP11 27 D2
Teasel Clo. SP11 27 C3
Tidworth Rd. SP11 27 A4

Saxifrage Bank. SN12 32 D4
Scotland Rd. SN12 32 B2
Semington Rd. SN12 32 B6
Severn Rd. SN12 32 B1
Shelley Clo. SN12 32 C4
Sherwood Av. SN12 32 D1
Short St. SN12 32 D1
Shurnhold. SN12 32 A2
Snarlton La. SN12 32 D3
Snowberry La. SN12 32 D5
Somerset Cres. SN12 32 C4
Sorrell Clo. SN12 32 C5
Southbrook Rd. SN12 32 A1
Spa Ct. SN12 32 B4
Spa Rd. SN12 32 B4
Speedwell Clo. SN12 32 C5
Spencer Clo. SN12 32 B1
Station App. SN12 32 A2
Strattons Walk. SN12 32 B3
Sweetbriar Rd. SN12 32 D4
Talbot Clo. SN12 32 D2
Tamar Rd. SN12 32 B1
Thackeray Cres. SN12 32 C3
Thames Cres. SN12 32 B1
The City. SN12 32 B2
The Close. SN12 32 C4
The Crays. SN12 32 D2
The Friars. SN12 32 D1
Thornbank. SN12 32 B4
Thornleigh. SN12 32 B3
Tower Rd. SN12 32 D3
Townsend Farm. SN12 32 B5
Trenchard Way. SN12 32 D6
Trent Cres. SN12 32 B1
Union St. SN12 32 B3
Vincent Clo. SN12 32 D3
Wardour Pl. SN12 32 B5
Warwick Cres. SN12 32 C4
Waverley Gdns. SN12 32 B5
Weavers Croft. SN12 32 B2
Wellington Dri. SN12 32 D6
Wellington Sq. SN12 32 C4
Wessex Vw. SN12 32 C4
West End. SN12 32 B4
Westbury Vw. SN12 32 D3
Western Way. SN12 32 A3
Wharf St. SN12 32 C4
Willow Clo. SN12 32 A4
Wiltshire Cres. SN12 32 C4
Windsor Av. SN12 32 C5
Winston Rd. SN12 32 A6
Woodcoombe. SN12 32 D1
Woodrow Rd. SN12 32 D1
Woodstock Gdns. SN12 32 B5

MERE

Angel La. BA12 28 B5
Ash Gro. BA12 28 C6
Barnes Pl. BA12 28 B5
Barton La. BA12 28 B5
Bishops Clo. BA12 28 B4
Boar St. BA12 28 B5
Bramley Hill. BA12 28 A5
Caddy La. BA12 28 A5
Castle Hill App. BA12 28 B5
Castle Hill Cres. BA12 28 B4
Castle Hill La. BA12 28 B5
Castle St. BA12 28 A5
Church La. BA12 28 B5
Church St. BA12 28 B5
Clements La. BA12 28 D6
Clews La. BA12 28 C5
Dark La. BA12 28 C5
Denes Av. BA12 28 B5
Downside Clo. BA12 28 C4
Hazzards Hill. BA12 28 A5
Home Field. BA12 28 A5
INDUSTRIAL & RETAIL:
  Quarryfield Ind Est.
    BA12 28 A5
  Woodlands Rd Ind Est.
    BA12 28 C6
Ivy Mead. BA12 28 C5
Jack Paul Clo. BA12 28 B4
Kingsmere Paddocks.
  BA12 28 A5
Long Hill. BA12 28 A5
Lordsmead Rd. BA12 28 C6
Lynch Clo. BA12 28 C6
Manor Rd. BA12 28 B4
Market Pl. BA12 28 B5
Mere By-Pass. BA12 28 A4
Mill La. BA12 28 C6

New Cut. BA12 28 C5
North Rd. BA12 28 B4
North St. BA12 28 B5
Nursery Gdns. BA12 28 C5
Old Hollow. BA12 28 C4
Penny Bank La. BA12 28 B5
Pettridge La. BA12 28 C5
Prospect Pl. BA12 28 A5
Queens Rd. BA12 28 C4
Salisbury St. BA12 28 B5
Shaftesbury Rd. BA12 28 C6
Southbrook. BA12 28 C6
Southbrook Gdns.
  BA12 28 D6
Spinners Way. BA12 28 C5
Springfield Rd. BA12 28 C5
Steep St. BA12 28 C4
The Drove. BA12 28 A5
The Fields. BA12 28 C4
The Lynch. BA12 28 C6
The Paddocks. BA12 28 C5
The Pound. BA12 28 C5
The Square. BA12 28 B5
The Yews. BA12 28 C4
Townsend Clo. BA12 28 B5
Underdown Mead.
  BA12 28 C4
Underhill. BA12 28 A5
Upper Water St. BA12 28 C5
Water St. BA12 28 C5
Wellhead. BA12 28 B4
White Rd. BA12 28 B5
Whitemarsh. BA12 28 C6
Woodlands Rd. BA12 28 C6

NORTH TIDWORTH

Abbots Clo. SP9 33 C2
Abbots Rd. SP9 33 C2
Adampur Rd. SP9 33 A4
Agra Rd. SP9 33 B4
Ash Clo. SP9 33 F2
Ashdown Ter. SP9 33 D4
Auckland Clo. SP9 33 F2
Avon Rd. SP9 33 C3
Baroda Rd. SP9 33 B4
Bazaar Rd. SP9 33 B4
Beech Hill Rd. SP9 33 E1
Bishops Clo. SP9 33 D4
Bourne Rd. SP9 33 E3
Bourne Vw. SP9 33 E1
Bulford Rd. SP9 33 B4
Cabul Rd. SP9 33 B4
Cherry Tree Av. SP9 33 E1
Chestnut Av. SP9 33 E1
Church La. SP9 33 D4
Churchill Clo. SP9 33 C1
Collins Ct. SP9 33 C1
Coronation Rd. SP9 33 D1
Dasna Rd. SP9 33 B3
Daunch Clo. SP9 33 C1
Dunedin Clo. SP9 33 F2
Ebble Clo. SP9 33 D2
Falcon Clo. SP9 33 E2
Forest Dri. SP9 33 E2
Furse Hill Rd. SP9 33 D4
Gason Hill Rd. SP9 33 C1
George VI Rd. SP9 33 D1
Gisborne Clo. SP9 33 E3
Grand Trunk Rd. SP9 33 A4
Hawthorn Rd. SP9 33 F2
Hill Top Av. SP9 33 C1
Humber La. SP9 33 C4
Iamrud Rd. SP9 33 C3
Jagdalik Rd. SP9 33 C4
Karachi Clo. SP9 33 C1
Kennet Rd. SP9 33 E2
Kestral Clo. SP9 33 E2
Kirklee Clo. SP9 33 C3
Kohat Clo. SP9 33 C2
Kohat Rd. SP9 33 C4
Lady Godley Clo. SP9 33 D3
Lahore Clo. SP9 33 C1
Lahore Rd. SP9 33 D3
Lark Clo. SP9 33 E2
Lowa Rd. SP9 33 C3
Ludgershall Rd. SP9 33 D2
Manor Bridge Ct. SP9 33 D1
Maple Ter. SP9 33 E2
Margha Rd. SP9 33 C2
Martin Clo. SP9 33 E2
Meerut Rd. SP9 33 C3
Mill Hill Av. SP9 33 D1

Monks Clo. SP9 33 D2
Nadder Clo. SP9 33 D2
Naini Tal Rd. SP9 33 C2
Napier Clo. SP9 33 F2
Nepaul Rd. SP9 33 C2
Oak Clo. SP9 33 F2
Ordnance Rd. SP9 33 D2
Paget Clo. SP9 33 C1
Park Rd. SP9 33 D3
Plantation Rd. SP9 33 D4
Pennings Rd. SP9 33 D1
Peshawar Clo. SP9 33 B1
Pheasant Clo. SP9 33 E2
Pinetree House. SP9 33 E2
Plassey Rd. SP9 33 C2
Raven Clo. SP9 33 E3
Rosewood Ct. SP9 33 E2
St Andrews Rd. SP9 33 D2
St Georges Rd. SP9 33 D3
St Michaels Av. SP9 33 C3
St Patricks Av. SP9 33 C3
Sidbury Circular Rd.
  SP9 33 C1
Sidbury Hill Av. SP9 33 D1
Station Rd. SP9 33 D3
Swallow Clo. SP9 33 E3
Sycamore Clo. SP9 33 F2
The Mall. SP9 33 A4
The Oval. SP9 33 D3
Vockins Clo. SP9 33 D4
Wavell Rd. SP9 33 C1
Wellington Rd. SP9 33 E2
Woodcock Clo. SP9 33 E3
Wylye Rd. SP9 33 D2
Zouch Av. SP9 33 C2
Zouch Clo. SP9 33 C2
Zouch Farm Rd. SP9 33 D2

PEWSEY

Astley Clo. SN9 34 C1
Aston Clo. SN9 34 B2
Avon Pl. SN9 34 B2
Avonleaze Rd. SN9 34 B1
Bailey Clo. SN9 34 A1
Ball Rd. SN9 34 C2
Bramley Clo. SN9 34 B1
Broadfields. SN9 34 A2
Broomcroft Rd. SN9 34 B1
Brunkards La. SN9 34 C1
Buckleaze La. SN9 34 B1
Cherry Clo. SN9 34 C1
Church St. SN9 34 B2
Coronation Clo. SN9 34 B2
Dursden La. SN9 34 C1
Easterton La. SN9 34 C2
Edwardian Ct. SN9 34 B1
Everleigh Rd. SN9 34 B3
Frensham Way. SN9 34 B3
Goddard Rd. SN9 34 B1
Green Drove. SN9 34 B3
Haines Ter. SN9 34 A2
Hawthorn Clo. SN9 34 B2
High St. SN9 34 B2
Holly Clo. SN9 34 C1
Holly Tree Wk. SN9 34 B2
Hollybush La. SN9 34 C1
INDUSTRIAL & RETAIL:
  Fordbrook Ind Est.
    SN9 34 B1
Inlands Clo. SN9 34 B1
King Alfred Clo. SN9 34 B1
Kings Corner. SN9 34 C2
Lime Clo. SN9 34 C1
Little Island. SN9 34 A1
Manningford Rd. SN9 34 A1
Manor Ct. SN9 34 B2
Maple Clo. SN9 34 C1
Market Pl. SN9 34 B2
Marlborough Rd. SN9 34 A1
Martinsell Grn. SN9 34 B1
Middlemass Grn. SN9 34 C1
Millennium Ct. SN9 34 B1
Milton Rd. SN9 34 C1
Nether Leaze. SN9 34 A1
North St. SN9 34 A1
Old Hospital Rd. SN9 34 A1
Phoenix Clo. SN9 34 B2
Raffin La. SN9 34 B3
Rawlins Rd. SN9 34 A2
River St. SN9 34 B2
Robinia Clo. SN9 34 C1
Rowan Clo. SN9 34 C1
St Johns Clo. SN9 34 C2

Salisbury Rd. SN9 34 A3
Scotchel Grn. SN9 34 B1
Slater Rd. SN9 34 B2
Southcott Rd. SN9 34 C2
Stratton Rd. SN9 34 B2
Swan Ct. SN9 34 B2
Swan Meadow. SN9 34 B3
Swan Rd. SN9 34 B2
The Crescent. SN9 34 A2
The Links. SN9 34 A2
The Square. SN9 34 A2
Tinkers Mead. SN9 34 C3
Vale Rd. SN9 34 A1
Walnut Clo. SN9 34 C1
Wheeler Clo. SN9 34 A1
Wilcot Rd. SN9 34 A1
Woodlands Rd. SN9 34 C3

POTTERNE

Blackberry La. SN10 34 C4
Blounts Ct. SN10 34 C6
Brownleaze La. SN10 34 C4
Court Hill. SN10 34 A6
Coxhill La. SN10 34 C6
Duck St. SN10 34 C5
Eastwell Rd. SN10 34 C5
Firs Hill Way. SN10 34 D4
High St. SN10 34 C5
Highlands. SN10 34 C5
Mill Rd. SN10 34 B5
Rookes La. SN10 34 C5
Ryeleaze. SN10 34 C4
St Marys Clo. SN10 34 D4
Silver St. SN10 34 D5
The Butts. SN10 34 C5
Tollbar Clo. SN10 34 C4
Whistley Rd. SN10 34 B4

SALISBURY

Abbot Rd. SP1 37 F4
Albany Rd. SP1 37 E6
Aldworth Dri. SP1 37 F3
Alexandra Clo. SP2 36 A5
Alexandra Dri. SP2 36 A5
Ancient Way. SP2 39 E4
Anderson Rd. SP1 37 F4
Andrews Way. SP2 38 D5
Angler Rd. SP2 35 D1
Apostles Way. SP1 37 F3
Ash Cres. SP1 37 F3
Ashfield Rd. SP2 38 B1
Ashlands. SP4 37 G2
Ashley Rd. SP2 36 C6
Assisi Rd. SP1 36 D3
Aston Mead. SP1 37 F5
Attwood Rd. SP1 37 E5
Australian Av. SP2 36 A6
Avon App. SP1 38 D1
Avon Ter. SP1 36 C6
Ayleswade Rd. SP2 38 D3
Ayrshrie Clo. SP2 35 D1
Balmoral Rd. SP1 37 E4
Barnard St. SP1 39 E2
Barnards Hill Dri. SP2 35 D2
Barrington Rd. SP1 37 F4
Bartlett Rd. SP1 37 E4
Beatrice Rd. SP1 39 F1
Becket Way. SP1 37 E5
Bedford Rd. SP2 36 C6
Bedwin St. SP1 39 E1
Beechcroft Rd. SP1 39 G1
Beeson Clo. SP2 38 C5
Bellamy La. SP1 39 F1
Belle Vue Rd. SP1 37 E6
Berkshire Rd. SP2 38 B3
Bingham Rd. SP1 37 F4
Bishopdown Rd. SP1 37 E5
Bishops Dri. SP2 38 C4
Bishops Mead. SP1 37 G4
Bishops Walk. SP1 38 D2
Blackfriars Way. SP1 39 E2
Blakey Rd. SP1 39 F2
Blandford Rd. SP2 38 A6
Blue Boar Row. SP1 38 D1
Blyth Way. SP1 37 F4
Bouchers Way. SP2 38 D5
Boundary Rd. SP1 37 H6
Bourne Av. SP1 37 F6
Bourne Clo. SP1 39 G2

Bourne Hill. SP1 39 E1
Bourne Way. SP1 39 G3
Bouverie Av. SP2 38 C5
Bouverie Av Sth. SP2 38 C5
Bouverie Clo. SP2 38 C5
Bower Gdns. SP1 39 F2
Bower Hill Rd. SP1 37 F6
*Bowes Lyon Ct,
  Philip Ct. SP2 36 A5
Braemar Rise. SP1 37 E4
Brick La. SP2 36 A6
Bridge St. SP1 38 D1
Britford La. SP2 39 E4
Britford La W. SP2 38 D3
Broad Wk. SP1 38 D2
Broadlands Clo. SP1 37 E4
Brown St. SP1 39 E1
Brunel Rd. SP2 38 B2
Burford Av. SP2 39 E4
Burford La. SP2 39 E4
Burford Rd. SP2 39 E4
Burgess Grn. SP1 37 F4
Burnett Way. SP1 37 F4
Butcher Row. SP2 38 D1
Butler Clo. SP2 39 E4
Butts Rd. SP1 36 D6
Byways Clo. SP2 39 F2
Cambridge Rd. SP1 37 E5
Campbell Rd. SP1 37 E6
Canadian Av. SP2 36 B6
Capulet Rd. SP1 36 C4
Carmelite Way. SP1 39 E3
Carrion Pond Drove.
  SP2 38 B4
Castle Keep. SP1 36 C4
Castle Rd. SP1 36 D2
Castle St. SP1 36 D6
Catherine St. SP1 39 E2
Cecil Av. SP2 38 D4
Cecil Ter. SP2 38 A1
Cedar Clo. SP2 35 D2
Centurion Clo. SP2 36 A5
Chancery Clo. SP2 36 B6
Charles St. SP2 36 C6
Charnwood Rd. SP2 36 B6
Chatham Clo. SP1 36 C4
Cherry Clo. SP2 36 B6
Cherry Orchard La. SP2 36 B6
Cheshire Clo. SP2 36 A4
Chestnut Clo. SP1 37 G5
Cheverell Av. SP1 37 F5
Chichester Clo. SP1 39 E4
Chipper La. SP1 38 D1
Chiselbury Gro. SP2 38 D4
Choristers Sq. SP1 38 D2
Christie Miller Rd. SP2 36 B6
Christopher Clo. SP2 38 C5
Church La. SP2 36 A6
Church La. SP5 39 G5
Church Rd. SP1 37 G6
Churchfields Rd. SP2 38 B1
Churchill Way East. SP1 37 E6
Churchill Way Nth. SP1 37 E4
Churchill Way Sth. SP1 39 E3
Churchill Way
  West. SP2 36 D6
Clarendon Rd. SP1 39 F1
Clifton Rd. SP2 36 C6
Coldharbour La. SP2 36 C6
College St. SP1 37 E6
Constable Way. SP2 38 C2
Cooks Clo. SP2 35 D1
Coombe Rd. SP2 38 B5
Cornwall Rd. SP1 36 D5
Coronation Rd. SP2 36 A5
Coronation Sq. SP2 35 B4
Courtwood Clo. SP1 39 F2
Cow La. SP1 37 F6
Crane St. SP1 38 D2
Cranebridge Rd. SP2 38 D1
Crestmount Dri. SP2 36 A5
Crown Ct. SP2 38 D3
Culver St. SP1 39 E2
Dairy Meadow La. SP1 39 G3
Dalewood Rise. SP1 37 G6
De Vaux Pl. SP1 38 D3
Denison Rise. SP1 37 F4
Devizes Rd. SP2 36 A3
Devonshire Rd. SP1 37 E5
Dews Rd. SP2 38 C1
Donaldson Rd. SP1 37 E5
Dorset Rd. SP1 37 E5
Douglas Haig Rd. SP1 36 D5
Down View Rd. SP1 37 G6

ownsway. SP1 37 E3	Hedley Davis Ct. SP2 38 B1	Milford Hollow. SP1 39 F2	Queen Alexandra Rd.	Skew Bridge Rd. SP2 36 A6
ryden Rd. SP2 39 E4	Herbert Rd. SP2 36 A5	Milford Manor Gdns.	SP2 36 A6	Skew Rd. SP2 35 C4
rake Clo. SP1 37 F3	Heronswood. SP2 38 D5	SP1 39 F2	Queen Manor Rd. SP1 39 G2	Smeaton Rd. SP2 38 B1
uck La. SP1 37 G6	High Rd. SP5 39 F5	Milford Mill Rd. SP1 39 G2	Queen Mary Rd. SP2 36 A4	Somerset Rd. SP1 37 E5
ublin Way. SP1 39 F2	High St. SP1 38 D2	Milford Pk. SP1 39 G2	Queen St. SP1 39 E1	South St. SP2 38 D1
unley Way. SP1 37 F3	Highbury Av. SP2 36 B6	Milford St. SP1 39 E1	Queens Rd. SP1 37 E6	South Western Rd. SP2 38 C1
urnford Rd. SP1 36 B1	Highbury Clo. SP2 36 B6	Mill La. SP1 36 B3	Queensberry Rd. SP1 36 D5	Southampton Rd. SP1 39 E2
	Highfield Rd. SP2 36 B6	Mill Rd. SP2 38 C1		*Spring Ct,
agle Field. SP2 36 A4	Highlands Rd. SP2 38 D4	Mill Stream App. SP1 38 D1	Radcliffe Rd. SP2 38 D4	Windsor Rd. SP2 38 C1
ast St. SP2 38 D1	Hill Rd. SP1 37 G6	Millbrook. SP1 39 F1	Radnor Rd. SP1 36 D4	Stanley Little Rd. SP2 35 C3
dgam Pl. SP2 35 B4	Hill Top Way. SP1 36 D3	Millennnium Clo. SP2 39 E5	Rambridge Cres. SP2 35 C2	Station Ter. SP2 38 B1
dison Rd. SP2 38 B1	Hill View Rd. SP1 39 E1	Millers Clo. SP1 36 B3	Ramleaze Dri. SP2 35 D1	Stephens Clo. SP2 38 B8
m Clo. SP1 37 G5	Hoadley Grn. SP1 37 G4	Milton Rd. SP2 38 C1	Rampart Rd. SP1 39 E1	Stephenson Rd. SP2 38 B1
m Ct. SP1 39 E1	Hollows Clo. SP2 38 C4	Minster St. SP1 38 D1	Ravenscroft. SP2 38 D5	Stockwood Clo. SP1 37 F5
m Gro. SP1 39 F1	Homington Rd. SP2 38 B6	Mitchell Rd. SP2 38 B6	Rawlence Rd. SP2 35 D3	Stratford Ct. SP1 36 D5
m Gro Pl. SP1 39 F1	Hudson Rd. SP1 36 C4	Moberly Rd. SP1 36 D5	Rectory Rd. SP2 38 C1	Stratford Rd. SP1 36 B2
m Gro Rd. SP1 39 E1	Hulse Rd. SP1 38 D5	Montague Rd. SP2 38 A3	Redford Clo. SP1 37 F5	Suffolk Rd. SP2 38 C3
mpire Rd. SP2 36 A6		Montgomery Gdns.	Richards Way. SP2 38 B3	Summerlock App. SP2 38 D1
ndless St. SP1 39 E1	India Av. SP2 36 B6	SP2 36 B6	Richmond Rd. SP2 36 C6	Sunnyhill Rd. SP1 37 F4
ssex Sq. SP2 38 B3	**INDUSTRIAL & RETAIL:**	Munks Clo. SP2 38 B3	Ridgeway Rd. SP1 37 E5	Sussex Rd. SP2 38 B4
stcourt Rd. SP1 37 E6	Churchfields Ind Est.	Myrrfield Rd. SP1 37 G3	Riverbourne Rd. SP1 39 G1	Swallow Mead. SP2 38 D5
veque Cl. SP2 35 B4	SP2 38 B1		Riverside Clo. SP1 37 G6	Swan Clo. SP2 38 D4
versglade. SP2 36 C6	Dolphin Trading Est.	Nadder La. SP2 35 B5	Riverside Rd. SP1 37 G6	Swaynes Clo. SP1 37 E6
xeter St. SP1 39 E3	SP1 39 F2	Nadder Ter. SP2 38 B1	Roberts Rd. SP2 36 A5	Swift Down. SP2 38 D4
eres Way. SP1 39 E2	Harnham Trading Est.	Napier Cres. SP1 39 G1	Rogers Clo. SP1 35 B4	Sycamore Dri. SP1 37 F3
	SP2 38 A3	Neal Clo. SP1 37 F2	Rollestone St. SP1 39 E1	Syringa Ct. SP2 38 A1
air View Rd. SP1 39 F1	Milford Trading Est.	Nelson Rd. SP1 36 D6	Roman Rd. SP2 36 A6	
air View Rd. SP2 35 A2	SP1 39 F2	Netheravon Clo. SP1 37 E5	Romer Rd. SP2 38 D4	Talbot Clo. SP1 37 F4
alcons Way. SP2 38 D5	Old Sarum Business Pk.	Netheravon Rd. SP1 37 E5	Rosemary Clo. SP1 37 G6	Telford Rd. SP2 38 B2
araday Rd. SP2 38 B1	SP4 37 E1	Netherhampton Rd,	Rosemary La. SP1 38 D2	The Avenue, Fugglestone
arley Rd. SP1 39 F2	Salisbury Business Pk.	Harnham. SP2 38 A3	Rougemont Clo. SP2 39 E1	St Peter. SP2 35 A3
arm La. SP2 38 B1	SP1 39 G3	Netherhampton Rd,	Rowan Clo. SP2 35 C3	The Avenue,
estival Av. SP2 35 D4	Salisbury Retail Pk.	Quidhampton. SP2 35 A6	Rowbarrow Clo. SP 39 E4	Laverstock. SP1 37 G6
eversham Rd. SP1 37 E4	SP1 37 G3	Neville Clo. SP1 37 F4	Russell Rd. SP2 36 B5	The Avenue,
nchley Rd. SP2 36 B6	The Bourne Centre.	New Bridge Rd. SP1 39 E3		Salisbury. SP1 39 F1
sh Row. SP1 39 E1	SP1 39 G3	New Canal. SP1 38 D2	St Albans Clo. SP1 37 G3	The Beeches. SP1 39 F2
sherton St. SP2 36 C6	Ivy St. SP1 39 E2	New Harnham Rd. SP2 38 A4	St Andrews. SP1 37 G6	The Brambles. SP1 37 F6
son Walk. SP1 37 G4		New St. SP1 38 D2	St Andrews Rd. SP2 36 A6	The Crusades. SP1 37 F3
olkestone Rd. SP2 38 C4	James St. SP2 36 C6	New Zealand Av. SP2 36 A6	St Ann Pl. SP1 39 E2	The Crescent. SP1 39 E1
olly Clo. SP2 38 C4	Jewell Clo. SP1 37 G4	Newton Rd. SP2 38 B1	St Ann St. SP1 39 E2	The Friary. SP1 39 E2
olly La. SP2 36 A5	*Jubilee Ct,	*Nightingale Walk,	St Bedes Clo. SP1 37 G3	*The Green,
olly View. SP2 35 D2	North St. SP2 38 D1	Christie Miller Rd. SP2 36 B6	St Brendans Clo. SP1 37 F3	Church Rd. SP1 37 G6
oots Hill. SP2 35 C4	Juniper Dri. SP1 36 D3	Norfolk Rd. SP2 38 B3	St Christophers Clo. SP1 37 F3	*The Hardings,
ord La. SP4 37 H2		North St. SP2 38 D1	St Clair Rd. SP1 39 E3	Devizes Rd. SP1 36 C6
otherby Cres. SP1 37 F4	Kelsey Rd. SP1 39 E1	North Walk. SP1 38 D2	St Clements Way. SP1 37 F3	The Kingsway. SP2 35 A2
owlers Hill. SP1 39 F2	Kensington Rd. SP2 36 C6	Norton Dri. SP4 37 G1	St Davids Clo. SP1 37 F3	The Maples. SP2 36 C6
owlers Rd. SP1 39 E2	Kent Rd. SP2 38 B3	Nursery Rd. SP2 36 B6	St Edmunds Church St.	The Meadows. SP1 39 G2
rancis Way. SP2 38 D5	Kingfisher Clo. SP2 38 D5		SP1 39 E1	The Oak Bournes. SP1 37 F3
riary La. SP1 39 E3	Kings Rd. SP1 37 E6	Oak Tree Field. SP2 39 E6	St Francis Cres. SP1 37 E3	The Orchard. SP1 37 F6
ugglestone. SP2 35 A3	Kingsland Rd. SP2 36 C6	Oakway Rd. SP1 37 E4	St Francis Rd. SP1 36 D4	The Portway. SP1 37 F3
	*Kivel Ct,	Odstock Rd. SP2 39 E5	St Georges Rd. SP2 38 A3	The Steadings. SP4 37 G2
ainsborough Clo. SP2 35 D3	Scamells Rd. SP1 36 D6	Old Blandford Rd. SP2 38 B5	St Gregory Av. SP2 36 A6	The Valley. SP2 35 D1
as La. SP2 36 C6		Old Castle Rd. SP1 36 D2	St James Clo. SP1 37 G3	Thistlebarrow Rd. SP1 36 D3
awthorne Dri. SP2 38 C3	Ladysmith Clo. SP2 36 A5	Old George Mall. SP2 38 D2	St John St. SP1 39 E1	Thompson Clo. SP2 38 C5
eorge St. SP2 36 C6	Laverstock Clo. SP1 37 G6	Old Meadows Walk.	St Johns Clo. SP2 39 G2	Tollgate Rd. SP1 39 E2
eorge St Sth. SP2 38 D1	Laverstock Pk W. SP1 37 G6	SP2 38 B3	St Josephs Clo. SP1 37 F3	Tournament Rd. SP2 36 A5
ibbs Clo. SP1 37 F3	Laverstock Rd. SP1 39 F1	Old Shaftesbury Drove.	St Judes Clo. SP1 37 G3	Tower Mews. SP1 37 E6
igant St. SP1 39 E2	Lees Ct. SP2 38 D1	SP2 38 A5	St Lawrence Clo. SP1 37 G3	Town Path. SP2 38 C2
ilbert Way. SP1 37 F4	Lime Kiln Way. SP2 38 D5	Old St. SP2 38 D4	St Lukes Clo. SP1 37 G3	Trinity St. SP1 39 E2
ilendale Cres. SP1 39 G1	Linden Clo. SP1 39 G1	Oldfield Rd. SP1 37 F3	St Margarets Clo. SP1 39 F2	Tryhorn Dri. SP1 37 F3
lenmore Rd. SP1 37 F5	Link Way. SP1 37 F5	Olivier Clo. SP1 35 D1	St Marks Av. SP1 37 E6	Turner Clo. SP2 38 B3
lyndebourne Clo. SP2 35 D3	Linnetsdene. SP2 38 D5	Orchard Pl. SP2 36 A6	St Marks Rd. SP1 37 E6	Tylers Clo. SP1 38 B3
odley Rd. SP2 38 D4	Locks La. SP2 35 B4	Orchard Rd. SP2 36 A6	St Martins Church St.	
orringe Rd. SP2 36 B6	London Rd. SP1 37 F6	Owls Wood. SP2 38 D5	SP1 39 E2	Upper St. SP2 38 B3
race Clo. SP2 35 D1	Longhill Dri. SP1 39 E4		St Marys Rd. SP2 38 C3	
ramshaw Rd. SP2 36 A6	Longland. SP2 36 B6	Paddock Way. SP1 37 H6	St Matthews Clo. SP1 37 G3	*Vanessa Av,
range Gdns. SP1 37 F6	Love La. SP1 39 E2	Palmer Rd. SP2 36 B6	St Michaels Rd. SP1 36 A4	The Avenue. SP1 37 G6
rasmere Clo. SP2 38 D4	Lovett Grn. SP1 37 F4	Park Clo. SP1 37 G6	St Michaels Rd. SP2 35 D2	Ventry Clo. SP1 37 E5
reen La. SP4 37 G1	Lower Rd. SP5 39 G6	Park La. SP5 39 G6	St Nicholas Rd. SP1 38 D3	Verona Rd. SP1 36 C3
reen Lane Clo. SP4 37 G2	Lower Rd. SP2 35 B4	Park Clo. SP1 36 D4	St Osmonds Clo. SP1 38 D3	Victoria Ct. SP1 36 D4
reencroft St. SP1 39 E1	Lower St. SP2 35 D2	Park La. SP1 36 D5	St Pauls Rd. SP1 38 C1	Victoria Dri East. SP2 39 E6
reenwood Av. SP1 39 G1	Lumley Clo. SP1 37 F3	Park Rd. SP1 37 G6	St Peters Rd. SP1 37 F3	Victoria Rd. SP1 36 D5
reyfriars Clo. SP1 39 E2		Park St. SP1 37 E6	St Teresas Clo. SP1 37 F3	Viking Way. SP2 39 E4
uilder La. SP1 39 E1	Macklin Av. SP2 36 B5	Parsonage Clo. SP1 36 B3	St Thomas Way. SP1 37 F3	
ypsy La. SP1 39 H2	Mallard Clo. SP1 38 C3	Parsonage Grn. SP2 38 C3	St Ursulas Clo. SP1 37 F3	Wain-a-long Rd. SP1 37 F6
	Malthouse La. SP2 38 D1	Pauls Dene Cres. SP1 37 E3	Salisbury Rd. SP2 35 A3	Warwick Clo. SP1 36 D5
adrians Clo. SP2 36 A4	Manning Clo. SP1 37 F2	Pauls Dene Rd. SP1 36 D3	Salt La. SP1 39 E1	Waterloo Rd. SP1 39 F2
allum Clo. SP1 37 G4	Manor Farm Rd. SP1 39 F1	Paynes Hill. SP1 39 E2	Sarum Clo. SP2 36 B5	Waters Rd. SP1 37 F4
amilton Rd. SP1 36 D6	Manor Rd. SP1 39 F1	Pearce Way. SP1 37 F2	Saxon Rd. SP2 38 C3	Watersmeet Rd. SP2 38 D3
ampton Ct. SP2 35 B4	Maple Cres. SP2 35 A3	Pembroke Rd. SP2 35 D4	Scamells Rd. SP1 36 D6	Watt Rd. SP2 38 D4
arcourt Ter. SP2 38 D1	Maplecroft. SP2 38 D4	Penning Rd. SP2 35 C3	Scots La. SP1 38 D1	Wavel Rd. SP2 38 D4
arnham Rd. SP2 38 C3	Marina Rd. SP1 39 F2	Pennyfarthing St. SP1 39 E1	Senior Dri. SP2 39 E4	Wellington Way. SP1 37 G6
arnwood Rd. SP2 38 C4	Marlborough Rd. SP1 37 E6	Penruddock Clo. SP2 35 D3	Seth Ward Dri. SP1 37 F5	Wessex Rd. SP1 39 F1
arper Rd. SP2 36 B6	Marsh La. SP2 36 C6	Peters Finger Rd. SP1 39 H3	Shady Bower. SP1 39 F2	West End Rd. SP2 36 B6
artington Rd. SP2 36 C6	Maryland Clo. SP1 35 C2	Philip Ct. SP1 36 A5	Shady Bower Clo. SP1 39 F2	West St. SP2 38 D2
artley Way. SP1 37 F3	Mayfair Rd. SP1 39 G1	Phillips La. SP1 36 B1	*Shakespeare Pl,	West Walk. SP1 38 D2
arvard Clo. SP2 38 D5	Meadow Rd. SP2 36 C6	Pilgrims Mead. SP1 37 F3	Windsor St. SP2 38 C1	Westbourne Clo. SP1 36 C6
atches La. SP1 39 G3	Meadow Rd Sth. SP2 36 C6	Pinewood Clo. SP2 35 D1	Shakespeare Rd. SP2 38 C1	Western Way. SP1 35 C3
athaway Clo. SP1 38 D4	Melvin Clo. SP1 39 G1	Pinewood Way. SP2 35 C2	*Sharrat Av,	Westfield Clo. SP1 37 G6
awks Ridge. SP2 38 D4	Merrifield Rd. SP4 37 F3	Polden Rd. SP1 39 F2	Ash Cres. SP1 37 F3	Westminster Rd. SP2 36 C6
*Hawthorn Clo,	Methuen Dri. SP1 39 E2	Poplar Way. SP1 37 F3	Sheen Clo. SP2 35 D1	Westwood Rd. SP2 35 D1
Wilton Rd. SP2 36 C6	Meyrick Av. SP1 39 E2	Portland Av. SP1 39 G1	Shelley Dri. SP1 36 C4	Whitbred Rd. SP2 35 D1
azel Clo. SP2 35 C3	Middle St. SP1 38 B2	Potters Way. SP1 39 G1	Shropshire Clo. SP2 35 D2	Whitebridge Rd. SP1 39 E2
eath Rd. SP2 36 A4	Middleton Rd. SP1 36 D6	Primrose Rd. SP2 36 A4	Sidney St. SP2 36 C6	Whitefriars Way. SP1 39 E2
	Milford Hill. SP1 39 E2	Pullman Dri. SP1 35 C4	Silver St. SP1 38 D1	*William Clo,
			Silverwood Dri. SP1 37 H5	Riverside Rd. SP1 37 G6

Willow Clo. SP1 37 G6
Wilman Way. SP2 38 C5
Wilton Rd,
  Quidhampton. SP2 35 B3
Wilton Rd. SP2 36 A6
Wiltshire Rd. SP2 38 B3
Winchester St. SP1 39 E1
Winding Way. SP2 35 D3
Windlesham Rd. SP1 37 E4
Windsor Rd. SP2 38 C1
Windsor St. SP2 38 C1
Wolferston Dri. SP1 37 G3
Woodbury Gdns. SP2 39 E4
Woodford Rd. SP2 36 A1
Woodland Way. SP1 37 G6
Woodside Rd. SP2 35 D3
Woodstock Rd. SP1 37 E6
Woodville Rd. SP1 37 F4
Wordsworth Rd. SP1 37 E6
Wrenscroft. SP2 38 D5
Wylye Clo. SP2 35 B4
Wyndham Rd. SP1 36 D6
Wyndham Ter. SP1 37 E6

York Rd. SP2 36 C6

SWINDON

Abbey View Rd. SN2 41 E3
Abington Way. SN2 42 B2
Abney Moor. SN3 47 G5
Acacia Gro. SN2 41 H4
Acorn Clo. SN3 47 E3
Aden Ct. SN2 41 F1
Addison Cres. SN2 42 C3
Adwalton Clo. SN5 44 B4
Affleck Clo. SN3 44 C3
Ainsworth Rd. SN3 46 D4
Akenfield Clo. SN2 41 F2
Akers Way. SN2 40 D4
Alanbrooke Cres. SN2 41 F5
Alba Clo. SN5 44 A1
Albert St. SN1 46 A4
Albion St. SN1 45 G3
Aldborough Clo. SN5 44 C1
Aldbourne Clo. SN2 41 H1
Alder Clo. SN2 40 D2
Alexandra Rd. SN1 45 H1
Alfred St. SN1 46 A1
Allington Rd. SN2 41 G1
Allison Ct. SN2 41 F4
Alnwick. SN5 44 C4
Alpine Clo. SN5 44 B1
Alton Clo. SN2 41 H1
Alvescot Rd. SN3 46 B3
Alveston Clo. SN5 44 D2
Amber Ct. SN1 46 B1
Amberley Clo. SN2 41 H3
Ambrose Rd. SN1 46 A5
Amersham Rd. SN3 47 E4
Amesbury Clo. SN2 41 H1
Ancona Clo. SN5 44 B1
Anderson Clo. SN3 47 F4
Andover St. SN1 45 F3
Angelica Clo. SN2 40 D3
Angler Rd. SN5 44 B1
Anglesey Clo. SN5 44 C2
Angus Clo. SN5 44 B1
Anise Clo. SN2 40 C3
Ansty Walk. SN2 41 G1
Applewood Ct. SN5 44 D3
Archers Clo. SN2 42 C1
Argyle St. SN2 42 A5
Arkwright Rd. SN2 42 A1
Arley Clo. SN2 41 F1
Arlington Clo. SN3 47 E1
Arliss Clo. SN2 41 G1
Armstrong St. SN1 46 A1
Arnfield Moor. SN3 47 G5
Arun Rd. SN2 41 F3
Arundel Clo. SN3 46 C4
Ascham Rd. SN5 44 B2
Ash Gdns. SN5 40 B5
Ash Gdns. SN3 43 G3
Ash Gro. SN2 41 H4
Ashburnham Clo. SN5 44 A4
Ashbury Av. SN3 47 E1
Ashford Rd. SN1 45 G3
Ashie Clo. SN5 40 C4
Ashington Way. SN5 44 C3
Ashkirk Clo. SN3 46 B2
Ashmore Clo. SN3 47 F2
Ashwell Clo. SN3 46 C3

Ashworth Dri. SN5 45 E2
Askerton Clo. SN5 40 A6
Askew Clo. SN5 44 A3
Atbara Clo. SN2 41 F3
Athena Av. SN2 42 B5
Attlee Cres. SN2 42 C3
Atworth Clo. SN2 41 G1
Auden Clo. SN2 41 E1
Audley Clo. SN5 44 A4
Austen Cres. SN3 47 F3
Avebury Rd. SN2 41 G2
Avening St. SN2 42 A6
Avens Clo. SN2 40 D2
Avenue Rd. SN1 46 A4
Avocet Clo. SN3 42 D2
Avonmead. SN2 41 E3
Axbridge Clo. SN3 46 D3
Aylesbury St. SN1 45 H1
Aymer Pl. SN3 47 E3
Ayrshire Clo. SN5 44 B1
Azelin Ct. SN3 43 E4

Babington Pk. SN5 44 A3
Bainbridge Clo. SN5 44 B3
Baird Clo. SN5 40 B6
Bakers Ct. SN3 43 E4
Bale Clo. SN5 44 A3
Balmoral Clo. SN3 46 D5
Bampton Gro. SN3 46 B2
Banbury Clo. SN3 46 C4
Bancroft Clo. SN5 44 A2
Bankfoot Clo. SN5 44 C1
Bankside. SN1 45 F4
Banwell Av. SN3 46 D3
Barbury Clo. SN2 41 E3
Barn Moor Clo. SN3 47 G4
Barnard Clo. SN3 47 E1
Barnfield Clo. SN2 45 E1
Barnfield Rd. SN2 45 E1
Barnstable Clo. SN3 46 D3
Barnstead Clo. SN5 44 B4
Barnum Ct. SN2 45 F1
Baron Clo. SN3 43 E3
Barrington Clo. SN3 47 G5
Barrowby Gate. SN3 42 D3
Barry Glen Clo. SN2 42 C5
Barton Rd. SN2 41 E3
Basil Clo. SN2 40 D3
Basingstoke Clo. SN5 44 B4
Baskerville Rd. SN3 47 G1
Bath Rd. SN1 45 H4
Bathampton St. SN1 45 G2
Bathurst Rd. SN1 46 A1
Baxter Clo. SN2 41 F1
Baydon Clo. SN2 41 E3
Bayleaf Av. SN2 40 D2
Beales Clo. SN1 45 H1
Beatrice St. SN2 41 H6
Beauchamp Clo. SN2 41 E3
Beaufort Grn. SN3 47 E3
Beaulieu Clo. SN5 44 D4
Beaumaris Rd. SN5 44 C3
Beaumont Rd. SN3 42 B6
Beckhampton St. SN1 46 A2
Beddington Ct. SN3 42 D2
Bedford Rd. SN3 46 C2
Bedwyn Clo. SN2 42 A4
Beech Av. SN2 41 F4
Beech Dri. SN5 40 B4
Beechcroft Rd. SN2 42 B3
Beehive Clo. SN5 40 A6
Belgrave St. SN1 46 A3
Bell Gdns. SN3 43 G3
Belle Vue Rd. SN1 46 A3
Bellver. SN5 44 C3
Belmont Clo. SN3 42 D3
Belmont Cres. SN1 45 G5
Belsay. SN5 44 C3
Belvedere Rd. SN3 46 D4
Bembridge Clo. SN3 47 E3
Bentley Clo. SN3 46 D2
Benwell Clo. SN5 44 C2
Berenger Clo. SN1 46 B4
Beresford Rd. SN3 47 F4
Bergman Clo. SN2 41 G1
Berkeley Lawns. SN3 46 C5
Berkshire Dri. SN5 44 B1
Berrington Rd. SN3 46 D4
Berry Copse. SN5 40 A5
Bess Rd. SN5 44 A4
Bessemer Clo. SN2 41 F5
Bessemer Rd East. SN2 41 F5
Bessemer Rd West.
  SN2 41 F5
Betony Clo. SN2 41 E2
Bevan Clo. SN2 42 C4

Beverley. SN5 44 C4
Beverstone Gro. SN3 46 C4
Bevil. SN5 44 B4
Bevisland. SN3 47 E4
Bibury Rd. SN3 46 B3
Bideford Clo. SN3 46 D3
Bindon Clo. SN5 44 A3
Birch St. SN1 45 F4
Birchwood Rd. SN3 43 E5
Birdbrook Rd. SN2 42 C2
Birdcombe Rd. SN5 44 C2
Bishopdale Clo. SN5 40 B6
Bisley Clo. SN3 46 B6
Bittern Rd. SN3 42 D2
Blackmore Clo. SN3 47 G1
Blackstone Av. SN3 47 F3
Blackthorn La. SN3 41 G3
Blake Cres. SN3 43 E4
Blakeney Av. SN3 47 E1
Blakesley Clo. SN3 46 D4
Blandford Ct. SN3 47 E2
Bletchley Clo. SN3 47 F4
Blockley Rise. SN3 42 D2
Bloomsbury Clo. SN5 44 B3
Blunsdon Rd. SN2 41 E1
Bodiam Dri. SN5 44 D3
Bodiam Dri North. SN5 44 D3
Bodiam Dri South. SN5 44 D4
Bodmin Clo. SN3 46 C4
Boldrewood. SN3 47 F4
Boleyn Clo. SN5 44 A2
Bolingbroke Rd. SN2 41 E4
Bonner Clo. SN5 44 D2
Borage Clo. SN2 40 D2
Boscombe Rd. SN2 41 E3
Bosham Clo. SN5 44 C3
Bosworth Rd. SN5 44 B2
Bothwell Rd. SN3 46 C1
Botley Copse. SN5 40 B4
Boundary Clo. SN3 42 C1
Bourne Rd. SN2 41 E4
Bourton Av. SN3 43 E5
Bouverie Av. SN3 46 B4
Bowden Clo. SN2 41 F2
Bowles Rd. SN2 41 F2
Bowleymead. SN3 47 F2
Bowling Green La. SN1 46 A5
Bowman Clo. SN3 43 E4
Boydell Clo. SN5 40 B6
Bradenham Rd. SN5 44 A3
Bradford Rd. SN1 46 A4
Bradley Rd. SN2 42 B3
Bradwell Moor. SN3 47 G5
Braemar Clo. SN3 46 B5
Bramble Clo. SN2 42 B5
Bramble Rd. SN2 42 C5
Bramdean Clo. SN2 41 F1
Bramwell Clo. SN2 42 C1
Brandon Clo. SN5 44 B3
Branksome Rd. SN3 41 E3
Bratton Clo. SN2 41 G2
Braybrooke Clo. SN5 40 A6
Brecon Clo. SN3 46 C5
Brem Hill Clo. SN2 41 H2
Brendon Walk. SN3 47 E2
Briar Fields. SN1 46 B1
Bridge End Rd. SN3 42 C6
Bridge St. SN1 45 G2
Bridgeman Clo. SN3 43 E4
Bridgemead Clo. SN5 44 D1
Bridgewater Clo. SN3 45 F1
Bridport Rd. SN3 46 D3
Briery Clo. SN3 42 D3
Bright St. SN2 42 B6
Brind Clo. SN3 47 G2
Brindley Clo. SN3 41 E6
Brington Rd. SN3 43 E6
Bristol St. SN1 45 G2
Britannia Pl. SN1 46 A4
Brixham Av. SN3 46 C3
Broad St. SN1 46 A1
Broadmead Walk. SN3 47 E1
Broadway. SN3 41 F3
Bromley Clo. SN3 46 C2
Bronte Clo. SN3 47 F4
Brook Lime Clo. SN2 40 D2
Brookdene. SN2 41 E2
Brooklands Av. SN3 41 F5
Brooks Clo. SN2 42 B2
Brooksby Way. SN3 43 E6
Broome Manor La. SN3 46 C5
Browning Clo. SN3 43 E3
Bruce St. SN2 45 F1
Bruddel Gro. SN3 46 B5
Brunswick St. SN1 45 H3

Bryanston Way. SN3 47 E2
Bryant Rd. SN2 40 C2
Bryony Way. SN3 40 D2
Buckhurst Cres. SN3 46 D2
Buckingham Rd. SN3 46 D5
Buckland Clo. SN3 46 D2
Bucklebury Clo. SN3 47 E1
Buckthorn Dri. SN2 40 D3
Buie Clo. SN5 40 C4
Buller St. SN3 42 B6
Bullfinch Clo. SN3 42 D2
Bunce Rd. SN3 42 D5
Burbage Rd. SN2 41 H1
Burden Clo. SN3 43 E5
Burford Av. SN3 46 B3
Burgess Clo. SN3 42 D5
Burghley Clo. SN3 46 D2
Burnet Clo. SN2 40 D2
Burnham Rd. SN3 46 D2
Burns Way. SN2 42 C3
Buttermere. SN3 47 G4
Butterworth St. SN1 45 F2
Byfield Way. SN3 43 E6
Byrd Clo. SN5 44 A3
Byron Clo. SN3 43 G2
Byron St. SN1 46 A3

Cabot Dri. SN5 44 A2
Cadley Clo. SN3 42 A4
Caen Vw. SN5 45 E3
Caernarvon Walk. SN3 46 C5
Cagney Dri. SN2 41 F1
Cairndow Way. SN2 42 B2
Calder Clo. SN2 41 F2
Callaghan Clo. SN3 42 D4
Callenders. SN5 44 C2
Calvert Rd. SN3 46 B2
Cambria Bri Rd. SN1 45 G2
Cambria Pl. SN1 45 G3
Cambridge Clo. SN3 46 C4
Camden Clo. SN5 44 A3
Cameron Clo. SN3 42 D5
Campden Rd. SN3 46 B3
Campion Gate. SN5 44 A2
Camton Rd. SN5 44 A1
Canal Walk. SN1 45 H1
Canford Clo. SN3 47 E2
Cannon St. SN1 46 A3
Canterbury Clo. SN3 46 C5
Capesthorne Dri. SN2 41 E1
Capitol Clo. SN3 43 F6
Caprice Clo. SN5 44 A1
Cardigan Clo. SN3 46 C4
Cardwell Clo. SN3 47 E1
Carey Clo. SN5 44 B3
Carfax St. SN1 45 H1
Carlisle Av. SN3 46 B4
Carlton Gate. SN3 46 D6
Carman Clo. SN3 43 E4
Carpenters La. SN2 42 B6
Carr St. SN1 45 G2
Carraway Dri. SN3 40 C3
Carroll Clo. SN3 47 F4
Carronbridge Rd. SN5 44 C2
Carshalton Rd. SN3 47 E4
Carslake Clo. SN3 47 E3
Carstairs Av. SN3 46 D4
Cartwright Dri. SN5 40 B6
Casson Rd. SN3 42 D5
Castilian Mews. SN5 44 B3
Castle Dore. SN5 44 B3
Castlefield Clo. SN3 44 C2
Castleton Rd. SN5 44 A1
Castleview Rd. SN3 46 C1
Catherine St. SN1 45 G2
Catherine Wayte Clo.
  SN2 41 F3
Catmint Clo. SN2 40 D3
Caulfield Rd. SN2 42 A6
Cavendish Sq. SN3 46 D4
Caversham Clo. SN3 46 D2
Cavie Clo. SN5 40 A6
Cawston Clo. SN3 46 C3

Chapel Rd. SN3 43 G
Chapel St. SN3 42 E
Charfield Clo. SN3 46 D
Charlbury Clo. SN3 41 E
Charles McPherson
  Gdns. SN3 47 F
Charlotte Mews. SN1 46 B
Charlton Clo. SN2 42 A
Charminster Clo. SN3 47 E
Charolais Dri. SN5 44 B
Chartley Grn. SN5 44 A
Chase Wood. SN5 40 A
Chatsworth Rd. SN2 41 F
Cheddar Rd. SN2 41 E
Chelmsford Rd. SN5 44 C
Cheltenham St. SN1 45 G
Chelworth Rd. SN2 41 E
Cheney Manor Rd. SN2 41 F
Chepstow Clo. SN5 44 C
Cheraton Clo. SN3 47 E
Cherhill Ct. SN2 41 E
Cherry Tree Gro. SN2 41 H
Chervil Clo. SN2 40 D
Chesford Clo. SN3 46 D
Chester St. SN1 45 G
Chesterfield Clo. SN5 44 C
Chestnut Av. SN2 42 A
Chevalier Clo. SN5 44 A
Cheviot Clo. SN5 44 B
Chickerell Rd. SN3 46 D
Chicory Clo. SN2 40 C
Chilton Gdns. SN2 41 E
Chilworth Clo. SN2 41 E
Chippenham Clo. SN3 41 G
Chippenham Way. SN2 41 G
Chives Way. SN2 40 D
Chobham Clo. SN3 42 D
Christie Clo. SN3 47 F
Chudleigh. SN5 44 B
Church Grnd. SN3 43 H
Church Pl. SN1 45 F
Church St. SN3 43 E
Church Walk. SN2 42 C
Church Walk Nth. SN2 41 F
Church Walk Sth. SN2 41 F
Church Way. SN3 42 D
Churchfield. SN2 41 E
Churchward Av. SN2 41 F
Cirencester Way. SN2 42 B
Clanfield Rd. SN3 47 E
Clare Walk. SN5 44 C
Clarence St. SN1 46 A
Clarendon La. SN5 45 F
Clarke Dri. SN5 50 B
Clary Rd. SN2 40 D
Clayhill Copse. SN5 40 A
Clays Clo. SN2 42 B
Cleasby Clo. SN5 44 D
Cleeve Lawns. SN1 46 C
Clevedon Clo. SN3 46 B
Cleves Clo. SN5 44 B
Clifton St. SN1 45 G
Clinton Clo. SN5 44 A
Cloche Way. SN2 42 C
Cloudberry Rd. SN2 41 E
Clouts Wood. SN5 40 B
Clover Lands. SN2 40 D
Clover Pk. SN2 40 D
Clydesdale Clo. SN5 44 B
Cobden Rd. SN2 41 F
Colbert Pk. SN2 41 F
Colbourne St. SN1 46 B
Colchester Clo. SN5 44 D
Cole Clo. SN3 47 F
Colebrook Rd. SN3 43 E
Coleridge Rd. SN3 41 E
College St. SN1 45 H
Collett Av. SN1 41 F
Collingsmead. SN3 47 F
Collins La. SN3 40 A
Colman Pk. SN2 41 F
Coln Cres. SN2 41 F
Colston Clo. SN3 46 D
Comfrey Clo. SN2 40 D
Commercial Rd. SN1 45 G
Commonweal Rd. SN1 45 G
Compton Clo. SN3 47 E
Conan Doyle Walk. SN3 47 G
Conisborough. SN5 44 C
Conrad Clo. SN3 47 F
Constable Rd. SN2 42 C
Constantine Clo. SN3 43 F
Conway Rd. SN3 42 C
Conyers Clo. SN5 44 A
Coombe Rd. SN2 41 E
Cooper Fld. SN2 41 F

ppice Clo. SN2 40 D3
pse Av. SN1 42 C6
rby Av. SN3 46 B5
rfe Clo. SN2 41 F3
rfe Rd. SN5 44 C3
riander Way. SN2 40 D2
rinium Way. SN3 43 F6
rnflower Rd. SN2 40 D2
rnmarsh Way. SN3 47 G1
rnwall Rd. SN2 41 G5
rporation St. SN1 46 A1
rral Clo. SN5 40 B6
rsham Rd. SN2 41 H2
rton Cres. SN5 44 C2
ttars Clo. SN3 43 E3
ttington Clo. SN5 44 B4
unty Rd. SN1 46 B1
urtenay Rd. SN3 46 D2
urtsknap Ct. SN1 45 F3
vingham Dri. SN3 43 F6
wdrey Clo. SN5 44 C4
wleaze Walk. SN2 42 C3
abtree Copse. SN5 40 B5
ampton Rd. SN3 46 D1
anborne Chase. SN2 40 C2
anmore Av. SN3 46 D4
awford Clo. SN5 44 B4
awley Av. SN3 43 E5
icklade Rd. SN2 42 A1
icklade St. SN1 46 B3
ieff Clo. SN3 47 E2
ispin Clo. SN3 43 E3
oftmead. SN1 45 H5
oft Rd. SN1 46 A6
ombey St. SN1 45 G2
ompton Rd. SN2 42 A1
omwell. SN5 44 B4
oss St. SN1 46 A3
ossways Av. SN2 41 H3
osswood Rd. SN3 46 D4
udwell Way. SN2 41 H1
ckoos Mead. SN3 47 G1
llerne Rd. SN3 43 F5
mberland Rd. SN3 46 B2
netio Rd. SN3 43 F6
nningham Rd. SN2 41 G4
rtis St. SN1 45 G3
press Gro. SN2 41 G4

cre Rd. SN3 46 D2
isy Clo. SN2 40 D3
lefoot Clo. SN5 40 A5
llas Av. SN3 47 E1
lton Clo. SN3 46 D1
lwood Clo. SN3 47 E4
mmas La. SN1 46 B4
nestone Clo. SN5 44 A1
rcey Clo. SN5 44 A2
rius Way. SN2 41 F1
rnley Clo. SN3 46 C2
rt Av. SN2 41 G3
rwin Clo. SN3 47 E1
venham Clo. SN3 46 D4
venwood. SN2 42 C2
wlish Rd. SN3 47 E2
y House La. SN3 47 E5
ys Clo. SN3 42 D5
acon St. SN1 45 G3
an St. SN2 45 F2
ben Cres. SN2 41 F2
burgh St. SN2 45 F2
erhurst Way. SN5 44 D3
lamere Dri. SN3 42 D3
nbeck Wood. SN5 44 C1
nbigh Clo. SN3 46 C4
nholme Rd. SN3 46 D4
nton Ct. SN3 43 E4
rby Clo. SN2 41 E5
rwent Dri. SN2 42 C2
sborough. SN5 44 B5
va Clo. SN3 43 F6
evereux Clo,
Grindal Clo. SN5 44 A3
vizes Rd. SN1 46 A4
von Rd. SN2 41 G5
wberry Clo. SN2 41 E2
well Mews. SN3 46 B4
xter Clo. SN5 44 B2
kens Clo. SN3 47 F4
kenson Rd. SN2 40 C2
more Rd. SN2 41 F1
on St. SN1 45 G3
bin Clo. SN3 47 G1
ckle Way. SN2 42 C3
n Clo. SN2 41 F2
nnington Gro. SN3 46 C4

Dorcan Way. SN3 47 E1
Dorchester Rd. SN1 46 C4
Dores Ct. SN2 42 B3
Dores Rd. SN2 42 B3
Douglas Rd. SN3 46 C2
Dover St. SN1 46 A3
Dovetrees. SN3 47 G1
Dowling St. SN1 45 H3
Downland Rd. SN2 40 D3
Downs View Rd. SN3 46 C6
Downton Rd. SN2 41 G2
Doyle Clo. SN2 40 C2
Drakes Way. SN3 46 C2
Draycott Clo. SN3 46 D2
Drew St. SN2 45 E1
Drove Rd. SN1 46 B3
Dryden St. SN1 45 G3
Duchess Way. SN2 42 B2
Dudley Rd. SN3 46 C2
Dudmore Rd. SN3 46 B2
Dukes Clo. SN2 42 B2
Dulverton Av. SN3 46 D3
Dunbarton Ter. SN1 46 A3
Dunbeath Rd. SN2 42 B5
Dunraven Clo. SN3 46 C4
Dunsford Clo. SN1 45 F3
Dunster Clo. SN3 46 C5
Dunwich Dri. SN5 44 D3
Durham St. SN1 46 A3
Durnford Rd. SN2 42 A2
Durrington Walk. SN2 41 H2

Eagle Clo. SN3 47 G1
Earl Clo. SN5 44 A1
East St. SN1 45 G2
Eastcott Hill. SN1 45 H3
Eastcott Rd. SN1 45 H3
Eastern Av. SN3 46 B2
Eastleaze Rd. SN5 44 C2
Eastmere. SN3 47 G4
Eastville Rd. SN2 41 H3
Eaton Clo. SN3 46 D4
Eaton Wood. SN5 40 A5
Eccleston Clo. SN3 47 E4
Ecklington. SN3 47 E3
Edale Moor. SN3 47 G5
Edgehill. SN5 44 B4
Edgeware Rd. SN1 45 H2
Edgeworth Clo. SN5 44 C1
Edinburgh St. SN2 42 A5
Edington Clo. SN5 44 C3
Edison Rd. SN3 47 F3
Edmund St. SN1 46 A3
Egerton Clo. SN3 47 E1
Elborough Rd. SN2 40 D3
Eldene Dri. SN3 47 E3
Elder Clo. SN2 40 D3
Elgin Dri. SN2 42 B5
Eliot Clo. SN3 47 G4
Elm Gro. SN5 40 B6
Elm Rd. SN2 41 F4
Elmina Rd. SN1 46 A1
Elmore. SN3 47 F2
Elmswood Clo. SN2 42 B2
Elsham Way. SN2 41 F2
Elsie Hazel Ct. SN5 44 B4
Elstree Way. SN2 41 F1
Ely Clo. SN5 44 D3
Emerson Clo. SN2 41 G1
Emlyn Sq. SN1 45 G2
Emmanuel Clo. SN2 41 F2
Enford Av. SN2 41 H1
Eric Long Clo. SN3 47 F3
Erlestoke Way. SN2 41 H1
Ermin St. SN3 42 C2
Espringham Pl. SN2 42 B2
Essex Walk. SN3 46 C2
Euclid St. SN1 46 A2
Euro Way. SN5 44 A5
Evelyn St. SN3 46 B5
Evergreens Clo. SN3 43 E5
Everleigh Rd. SN2 41 H2
Eworth Clo. SN5 44 A3
Exbury Clo. SN2 41 F1
Exe Clo. SN2 41 G2
Exeter St. SN1 45 G2
Exmouth St. SN1 45 G3

Fairfax Clo. SN3 46 C1
Fairford Cres. SN2 41 H3
Fairholme Way. SN2 42 C3
Fairlawn. SN3 47 F5
Fairview. SN1 45 G3
Falconscroft. SN3 47 F1
Falmouth Gro. SN1 46 C3
Fanstones Rd. SN3 47 E4
Faraday Rd. SN3 47 G3
Fareham Clo. SN3 47 E3
Faringdon Rd. SN1 45 G2
Farleigh Cres. SN3 46 C5
Farman Clo. SN3 47 F4
Farnborough Rd. SN3 46 D5
Farnsby St. SN1 45 G2
Farrfield. SN2 42 C3
Farriers Clo. SN1 42 B6
Feather Wood. SN5 44 D3
Fenland Clo. SN5 44 A1
Fennel Clo. SN2 40 D2
Ferndale Rd. SN2 41 F6
Fernham Rd. SN2 41 E4
Ferrers Dri. SN5 44 A3
Field Rise. SN1 45 G5
Fieldfare. SN3 47 F1
Finchdale. SN3 43 F6
Fir Tree Clo. SN2 41 F4
Firecrest Vw. SN3 47 G2
Firth Clo. SN2 41 F3
Fitzmaurice Clo. SN3 47 F1
Fitzroy Rd. SN1 46 A5
Fleet St. SN1 45 G2
Fleetwood Ct. SN5 44 B4
Fleming Way. SN1 45 H2
Flint Hill. SN5 44 C4
Florence St. SN2 41 H6
Folkestone Rd. SN1 45 G3
Fonthill Walk. SN3 46 C3
Ford St. SN1 45 F3
Forester Clo. SN3 47 G3
Forsey Clo. SN3 47 G1
Forum Clo. SN3 43 F6
Fosse Clo. SN2 45 E2
Fovant Clo. SN5 40 B5
Fowey. SN5 44 B4
Fox Hill Clo. SN2 41 F3
Foxbridge. SN3 47 G1
Foxglove Rd. SN2 40 D2
Foxley Clo. SN2 42 B3
Foxwood. SN5 44 D3
Frampton Clo. SN5 44 C2
Francomes. SN2 41 E2
Frankland Rd. SN5 44 A5
Frankton Gdns. SN3 43 E5
Fraser Clo. SN3 47 E1
Freshbrook Way. SN5 44 B3
Friesian Clo. SN5 44 B1
Friesland Clo. SN5 44 B1
Frilford Dri. SN3 42 D5
Frith Copse. SN5 40 B4
Frobisher Dri. SN3 46 C2
Frome Rd. SN2 41 F3
Fry Clo. SN5 45 F3
Fullers Clo. SN2 42 C2
Furlong Clo. SN2 41 E2
Furze Clo. SN5 40 B5
Fyfield Av. SN2 41 H1
Fyne Clo. SN5 40 C5

Gable Clo. SN2 41 G1
Gainsborough Way.
SN5 44 B4
Gairlock Clo. SN5 40 C4
Galloway Clo. SN5 44 B1
Galloway Rd. SN2 40 C2
Galsworthy Clo. SN3 47 G3
Gambia St. SN1 46 B2
Gantlett Dene. SN3 47 G2
Ganton Clo. SN2 42 C5
Ganton Way. SN2 42 C5
Garfield Clo. SN3 47 F4
Garrard Way. SN3 42 D6
Garside Grn. SN2 42 B2
Garson Rd. SN2 41 G1
Gartons Rd. SN5 44 A1
Gaynor Clo. SN2 41 F1
Gays Pl. SN2 42 C2
Gayton Way. SN3 43 E6
George St. SN1 45 F2
Gerard Walk. SN5 44 B2
Gibbs Clo. SN3 47 G1
Gifford Rd. SN3 43 E3
Gilberts Hill. SN1 45 H3
Gilling Way. SN3 47 G2
Gipsy La. SN2 42 B6
Gladstone St. SN1 46 A1
Glenmore Rd. SN2 40 C2
Glenwood Clo. SN1 46 A6
Glevum Rd. SN3 43 F6
Globe St. SN1 45 H3
Gloucester St. SN1 45 H1
Goddard Av. SN1 45 G4
Godolphin Clo. SN5 44 A4
Godwin Rd. SN3 43 E3
Goldcrest Walk. SN3 47 G1
Goldsborough Clo. SN5 44 C2
Gooch St. SN1 46 A1
Gordon Gdns. SN1 45 H2
Gordon Rd. SN1 46 A2
Goulding Clo. SN3 42 D4
Gower Clo. SN5 44 A3
Gower Clo. SN2 42 C4
Grafton Rd. SN2 42 A2
Graham St. SN1 46 A1
Grailey Clo. SN3 47 F4
Granary Clo. SN5 40 A6
Grandison Clo. SN5 44 A2
Grange Dri. SN3 42 D5
Grange Park Way. SN5 44 A3
Grantham Clo. SN5 44 B5
Grantley Clo. SN3 46 D4
Granville St. SN1 45 H2
Grasmere. SN3 47 G4
Graythwaite Clo. SN2 41 F1
Great Western Way.
SN5 44 A5
Green Hill Rd. SN2 41 E4
Green Meadow Av. SN2 41 F3
Green Rd. SN2 42 B3
Green Valley Av. SN2 41 F2
Greenbridge Rd. SN3 46 D1
Greenfields. SN3 43 G2
Greenlands Rd. SN2 42 C4
Greenway Clo. SN3 47 E1
Greenwich Clo. SN2 41 F2
Gresham Clo. SN3 46 C2
Greywethers Av. SN3 46 B4
Griffiths Clo. SN3 43 E5
Grindal Dri. SN5 44 A3
Grosmont Dri. SN5 44 B3
Grosvenor Rd. SN1 45 F4
Groundwell Av. SN1 46 A2
Grovelands Av. SN1 46 A5
Grovellly Clo. SN5 40 B5
Groves St. SN2 45 F2
Grundys. SN3 47 F4
Guildford Av. SN3 46 C5
Guppy St. SN2 45 F2

Hackett Clo. SN2 42 B2
Hackleton Rise. SN3 43 E6
Haddon Clo. SN5 44 A3
Hadleigh Clo. SN5 44 D2
Hadleigh Rise. SN3 42 D2
Hadrians Clo. SN3 43 F6
Haig Clo. SN2 42 B3
Hallam Moor. SN3 47 G5
Hamble Rd. SN2 41 F3
Hamilton Clo. SN3 46 C1
Hampshire Clo. SN5 44 B1
Hampton Dri. SN5 44 A2
Hamworthy Rd. SN3 47 F2
Hanbury Rd. SN3 46 D4
Handel St. SN2 41 H6
Hannington Clo. SN2 41 G1
Hanson Clo. SN5 44 B1
Harbour Clo. SN2 41 F3
Harcourt Rd. SN2 41 F6
Hardie Clo. SN3 42 D5
Harding St. SN1 45 G2
Hardwick Clo. SN2 41 F2
Hare Clo. SN2 42 C1
Harebell Clo. SN2 41 E2
Hargreaves Rd. SN2 42 B1
Harlech Clo. SN5 44 C4
Harlestone Rd. SN3 43 E6
Harptree Clo. SN5 40 A6
Harrington Walk. SN3 46 D1
Harris Rd. SN2 41 F5
Harrow Clo. SN3 42 D5
Hartland Clo. SN3 46 D3
Hartsthorn Clo. SN2 40 D3
Harvester Clo. SN5 40 A6
Harvey Gro. SN2 41 F5
Haslemere Clo. SN3 47 E4
Hatfield Clo. SN2 41 E1
Hathaway Rd. SN2 42 B2
Hatherall Clo. SN3 43 F5
Hatherley Rd. SN3 47 E1
Hathersage Moor. SN3 47 G5
Hatton Gro. SN3 46 C2
Havelock St. SN1 45 H2
Haven Clo. SN3 43 E6
Hawker Rd. SN3 47 E3
Hawkfinch Clo. SN3 47 G2
Hawkins St. SN2 45 F1
Hawkswood. SN3 43 F6
Hawksworth Way. SN2 45 G1
Hawthorn Av. SN2 41 H4
Hay La. SN4 44 A6
Haydon Ct. SN2 41 E2
Haydon Court Dri. SN2 41 E2
Haydon End La. SN2 41 E1
Haydon St. SN1 45 H1
Haydon View Rd. SN2 41 H3
Haydonleigh Dri. SN2 41 E2
Haynes Clo. SN3 47 E4
Hayward Clo. SN2 41 G1
Hazebury Cres. SN3 47 F1
Hazel Gro. SN2 41 H3
Headlands Gro. SN2 42 B4
Heath Way. SN3 43 E6
Heathcote Clo. SN5 40 B6
Heaton Clo. SN2 41 F1
Heddington Clo. SN2 41 H2
Hedgerow Clo. SN3 47 E3
Hedges Clo. SN3 43 E4
Helmsdale. SN2 41 E3
Helston Rd. SN3 46 D3
Henley Rd. SN3 46 D4
Henman Clo. SN2 41 F2
Henry St. SN1 45 G2
Hepworth Rd. SN2 41 F1
Hereford Lawns. SN3 46 C5
Hermitage La. SN2 42 B3
Heronbridge Clo. SN5 44 C2
Heronscroft. SN3 47 F1
Hertford Clo. SN3 46 C2
Hesketh Cres. SN3 46 A5
Hewitt Clo. SN3 47 F4
Hexham Clo. SN5 44 B3
Heytsbury Gdns. SN5 44 A4
Heywood Clo. SN2 41 G2
High St. SN2 41 E2
High St. SN1 46 B4
Highclere Av. SN3 46 C4
Highland Clo. SN5 44 B1
Highmoor Copse. SN5 40 A5
Highnam Clo. SN3 42 D5
Highwood Clo. SN2 40 D3
Highworth Rd. SN3 42 D3
Hill View Rd. SN3 43 F6
Hillary Clo. SN2 41 H3
Hillcrest Clo. SN1 45 G4
Hillingdon Rd. SN3 47 E4
Hillmead Dri. SN5 40 B6
Hillside Av. SN1 45 G4
Hillyard Clo. SN5 44 A3
Hilmarton Av. SN2 41 H1
Hinton St. SN2 42 B6
Hobley Dri. SN3 42 D4
Hodds Hill. SN5 40 B4
Holbein Field. SN5 44 B3
Holbein Mews. SN5 44 B3
Holbein Pl. SN5 44 B3
Holbein Walk. SN5 44 B3
Holbrook Way. SN1 45 G2
Holden Cres. SN2 41 G1
Holliday Clo. SN2 41 F1
Holinshed Pl. SN5 44 B3
Hollins Moor. SN3 47 G5
Holly Clo. SN2 41 F4
Holmleigh. SN2 41 E3
Honeylight Vw. SN2 41 F1
Honeysuckle Clo. SN2 40 D2
Honiton Rd. SN3 47 E3
Hook St. SN5 44 A4
Hoopers Pl. SN1 46 B4
Hopton Clo. SN5 44 C4
Horace St. SN2 45 F2
Horcott Rd. SN5 40 B4
Hornsey Gdns. SN3 42 D2
Horsham Cres. SN3 46 D3
Horseshoe Clo. SN5 40 A5
Horton Rd. SN2 42 C1
Howard Clo. SN3 46 C2
Huddleston Clo. SN2 42 B6
Hudson Way. SN2 41 F2
Hughes St. SN2 45 E1
Hugo Way. SN2 41 G1
Hungerford Clo. SN5 44 A1
Hunsdon Clo. SN3 46 D2
Hunt St. SN1 46 A3
Hunters Gro. SN2 41 G5
Huntley Clo. SN3 46 C1
Hunts Rise. SN3 43 E1
Hurst Cres. SN2 41 H4
Hyde Rd. SN2 42 B1
Hylder Clo. SN2 40 D3
Hysopp Clo. SN2 40 C3
Hythe Rd. SN1 45 H3

Icomb Clo. SN5 44 C4
Idovers Dri. SN5 44 C3
Iffley Rd. SN2 41 F6
Imber Walk. SN2 41 G1

INDUSTRIAL & RETAIL:

Axis Business Centre. SN5 44 D1
Blagrove Employment Area. SN5 44 A5
Britannia Trade Pk. SN3 42 C4
Cheney Manor Ind Est. SN2 41 E5
Churchward Pk. SN5 45 E3
Delta Business Pk. SN5 44 D2
Dorcan Ind Est. SN3 47 G3
Elgin Ind Est. SN2 42 B5
Europa Pk Employment Area. SN3 42 D4
Greenbridge Ind Est. SN3 42 D6
Groundwell Ind Est. SN2 42 B1
Hawksworth Ind Est. SN2 45 F1
Headlands Ind Est. SN2 42 B4
Hillmead Employment Area. SN5 40 B6
Honda Car Plant. SN3 43 E2
Isis Trading Est. SN1 42 C6
Kembrey Business Pk. SN2 42 B5
Kendrick Ind Est. SN2 41 E6
Mannington Employment Area. SN5 45 E3
Marshgate Ind Est. SN1 42 C6
Okus Ind Est. SN1 45 G4
Rivermead Ind Est. SN5 40 C6
Techno Trading Est. SN2 42 C5
Thornhill Ind Est. SN3 43 G3
Transfer Bridge Ind Est. SN2 42 B6
Westmead Ind Est. SN5 44 D1
Windmill Hill Business Pk. SN5 44 A4
Inglesham Rd. SN2 41 H2
Ipswich St. SN2 41 H6
Irston Way. SN5 44 B4
Isis Clo. SN2 41 G3
Islandsmead. SN3 47 F3
Islington St. SN1 45 H2
Ixworth Clo. SN5 44 B1

*Jack Thorne Clo, Linden Way. SN5 40 B4
Jacobs Walk. SN3 47 G3
James Watt Clo. SN5 45 F1
Jasmine Clo. SN2 40 D3
Jefferies Av. SN2 42 B4
Jennings St. SN2 45 F2
Jersey Pk. SN5 44 B1
Jewel Clo. SN5 44 A3
John Herring Cres. SN3 42 D5
John St. SN1 45 H2
Jole Clo. SN2 42 C2
Jolliffe St. SN1 45 F2
Joseph St. SN1 45 G3
Jubilee Clo. SN2 40 D4
Juliana Clo. SN5 44 B1
Juniper Clo. SN3 43 E6

Keats Cres. SN2 42 C3
Keble Clo. SN3 47 E1
Kelham Clo. SN3 46 C4
Kelly Gdns. SN2 41 F1
Kelmscot Rd. SN2 41 H3
Kelvin Rd. SN3 46 D1
Kemble Dri. SN5 45 F1
Kembrey St. SN2 42 A5
Kendal. SN5 44 B5
Kenilworth Lawns. SN3 46 C5
Kennedy Dri. SN3 47 F4
Kennet Av. SN2 41 G3
Kent Rd. SN1 45 G3
Kenton Clo. SN3 47 E2
Kenwin Clo. SN3 43 E4
Kerry Clo. SN3 44 B2
Kershaw Rd. SN3 47 F4
Kestrel Dri. SN3 47 G2
Keswick Rd. SN3 47 E4
Keycroft Copse. SN5 40 A5
Keynesham Rd. SN3 47 F2

Keynsham Walk. SN3 47 E4
Kilben Clo. SN5 44 A1
Kiln La. SN2 41 F5
Kilsby Way. SN3 43 E6
Kilsyth Clo. SN5 44 B3
Kimberley Rd. SN3 46 D4
Kimbolton Clo. SN5 44 B4
Kimmeridge Clo. SN3 47 E2
King Charles Rd. SN5 44 B4
King Henry Dri. SN5 44 A3
King John St. SN1 46 A3
King St. SN1 45 H2
King William St. SN1 46 A3
Kingfisher Dri. SN3 47 F1
Kingscote Clo. SN5 40 A6
Kingsdown Rd. SN2 42 C2
Kingshill Rd. SN1 45 F3
Kingsley Way. SN2 42 B2
Kingsthorpe Gro. SN3 43 F6
Kingston Rd. SN3 46 D4
Kingsway Clo. SN3 46 D3
Kingswood Av. SN3 46 D3
Kipling Gdns. SN2 42 C3
Kirby Clo. SN3 46 C4
Kirkstall Clo. SN3 44 C3
Kirktonhill Rd. SN5 44 D2
Kitchener St. SN2 41 H6
Knapp Clo. SN2 41 F4
Knowsley Rd. SN3 46 D4

Laburnum Rd. SN2 41 H4
Lacock Rd. SN2 42 A2
Lady La. SN2 41 E1
Lagos St. SN1 46 A1
Lakeside. SN3 46 B4
Lambert Clo. SN5 44 B4
Lambourne Av. SN3 46 B5
Lamora Clo. SN5 40 A6
Lanac Rd. SN3 42 D6
Lancaster Mews. SN3 43 F1
Lancaster Pl. SN3 43 F1
Langdale Dri. SN5 44 B4
Langford Gro. SN3 46 B2
Langport Clo. SN5 44 B3
Langstone Way. SN5 44 C2
Lanhydrock Clo. SN5 44 B3
Lansbury Dri. SN2 42 C3
Lansdown Rd. SN1 45 H3
Lapwing Clo. SN3 47 G2
Larchmore Clo. SN3 41 G3
Larksfield. SN3 47 F1
Latton Clo. SN2 41 G1
Lawrence Clo. SN3 47 F3
Lawton Clo. SN3 47 F3
Leamington Gro. SN3 46 C5
Leicester St. SN1 46 A2
Leigh Rd. SN2 41 H2
Leighton Av. SN3 46 D4
Lennox Dri. SN3 46 C2
Leslie Clo. SN5 44 B3
Lethbridge Rd. SN1 46 A4
Letterage Rd. SN5 40 B4
Leven. SN5 44 B5
Leverton Gate. SN3 46 C6
Lewisham Clo. SN2 41 E4
Lichen Clo. SN2 40 D3
Liddington St. SN2 42 A4
Liden Dri. SN3 47 F4
Limes Av. SN2 41 G4
Lincoln St. SN1 46 A2
Linden Av. SN2 41 H4
Linden Way. SN5 40 B4
Lineacre Clo. SN3 44 A4
Linley Clo. SN1 46 A5
Linnetsdene. SN3 43 F6
Linslade St. SN2 45 F2
Liskeard Way. SN5 44 B4
Lisle Clo. SN5 44 A3
Little Av. SN2 41 F5
Little London. SN1 46 A3
Littlecote Clo. SN5 44 B3
Locksgreen Cres. SN2 41 E3
Logan Clo. SN3 46 B2
Lomond Clo. SN5 40 C5
London St. SN1 45 H2
Longstock Ct. SN5 44 C2
Longthorpe Clo. SN5 44 D3
Loughborough Clo. SN3 44 A3
Louviers Way. SN1 46 A5
Loveage Clo. SN2 40 D3
Lovell Clo. SN3 47 F1
Loveridge Clo. SN2 42 B1
Lowes Clo. SN5 40 C4

Lucerne Clo. SN5 44 A1
Luddesdown Rd. SN5 44 C4
Ludlow Clo. SN3 46 C4
Lulworth Rd. SN2 41 E3
Lumley Clo. SN5 44 A3
Lyddon Way. SN2 41 F3
Lydford Clo. SN5 40 B6
Lyme Way. SN2 41 F2
Lyndhurst Cres. SN3 46 D2
Lyneham Clo. SN2 41 H1
Lynton Rd. SN2 41 E5
Lynwood Gro. SN2 40 D3
Lytchett Way. SN3 47 F2

Mackenzie Clo. SN3 47 G4
Magpie La. SN3 47 G1
Maidstone Rd. SN1 45 G3
Maitland Rd. SN3 46 D1
Majestic Clo. SN5 44 A1
Maldwyn Clo. SN5 44 A1
Mallard Clo. SN3 47 G2
Mallow Clo. SN2 40 D2
Malvern Rd. SN2 41 H5
Manchester Rd. SN1 45 H1
Mannington La. SN5 44 D3
Mannington Pk. SN5 45 E1
Manor Cres. SN2 41 E4
Manor Gdns. SN2 41 F5
Manor Pk. SN3 43 G3
Manor St. SN1 45 F3
Manton St. SN2 45 F1
Maple Gro. SN2 41 H4
March Clo. SN2 41 F1
Mardale Clo. SN5 40 A6
Margaret's Grn. SN3 43 E4
Marigold Clo. SN2 40 D2
Marjoram Clo. SN2 40 D2
Markenfield. SN5 44 D3
Market St. SN1 45 G2
Markham Clo. SN3 46 C1
Marlborough La. SN3 46 B5
Marlborough Rd. SN3 46 B4
Marlborough St. SN1 45 F3
Marlowe Av. SN3 46 D1
Marney Rd. SN3 47 F1
Marshall Rd. SN5 40 B6
Marshfield Way. SN3 42 D5
Marshgate. SN1 42 C6
Marsland Rd. SN2 42 B4
Marston Av. SN2 42 A2
Martinfield. SN3 47 F1
Masefield Av. SN2 42 B4
Matley Moor. SN3 47 G5
Maxey Clo. SN5 40 B6
Maxwell St. SN1 45 G2
May Clo. SN2 41 H5
Mayfield Clo. SN3 47 E1
Mead Way. SN5 44 C1
Meadow Rd. SN2 45 E1
Meadowcroft. SN2 42 C2
Meadowsweet Clo. SN2 41 E1
Meares Dri. SN6 40 B6
Medbury Rd. SN1 46 A2
Medina Way. SN2 42 C2
Medway Rd. SN1 41 F3
Melbourne Clo. SN3 46 D5
Melfort Clo. SN5 40 C5
Melford Walk. SN3 47 E1
Melksham Clo. SN3 41 G1
Mellow Ground. SN2 41 E2
Melrose Clo. SN3 44 C1
Melville Clo. SN3 46 C2
Melvyn Webb Pl. SN2 42 B6
Menham Clo. SN2 42 A4
Mendip Clo. SN2 41 H3
Merlin Way. SN3 43 F6
Merrivale Gro. SN1 46 B3
Merton Av. SN2 42 B3
Merton St. SN1 45 H2
Middleleaze Dri. SN5 44 A1
Middleton Clo. SN3 46 C2
Midhurst Av. SN3 47 E2
Midwinter Clo. SN5 40 B5
Midwinter Gdns. SN3 42 D4
Mildenhall Way. SN2 41 G1
Mildmay Clo. SN5 44 A3
Milford St. SN1 45 H2
Mill La. SN1 45 F5
Millbuck Clo. SN3 47 H3
Miller Clo. SN5 44 A1
Milston Av. SN2 45 F1
Milton Rd. SN1 45 G2
Minety Rd. SN2 41 G1
Mint Clo. SN2 40 D3
Monet Clo. SN5 44 A1
Monkton Clo. SN3 47 E4

Monmouth Clo. SN3 46 C4
Montagu St. SN2 45 E1
Monteagle Clo. SN5 44 A3
Montgomery Av. SN2 41 G5
Montrose Clo. SN2 41 E4
Moorhen Clo. SN3 47 G2
Moray Rd. SN2 42 B5
Moredon Pk. SN2 40 D3
Moredon Rd. SN2 41 E3
Moresby Clo. SN5 44 C2
Morie Clo. SN5 40 C5
Morley St. SN1 45 H2
Morris St. SN2 45 E2
Morrison St. SN2 45 E1
Morse St. SN1 45 G3
Mortimer Clo. SN5 44 C1
Mulberry Gro. SN2 41 F4
Mulcaster Av. SN5 44 A3
Mundy Av. SN3 47 E3
Munro Clo. SN3 46 B2
Murdoch Rd. SN3 47 G2
Myrtle Gdns. SN2 41 H4

Nantwich. SN5 44 B5
Napier Clo. SN3 45 F1
Naunton Rd. SN3 47 E3
Nelson St. SN1 45 F3
Ness Clo. SN5 40 C4
Netherton Clo. SN3 47 E4
Nevis Clo. SN5 40 C4
New Bridge Clo. SN1 45 H1
New Bridge Sq. SN1 45 H2
New Meadow Copse. SN5 40 B5
Newark Clo. SN5 44 A3
Newburn Cres. SN1 45 F3
Newbury Dri. SN5 44 A3
Newcastle St. SN1 46 A2
Newcome Dri. SN2 45 F1
Newhall St. SN1 45 H3
Newland Rd. SN2 41 F3
Newport St. SN1 46 A4
*Newstead Clo, Bicton Rd. SN2 41 F1
Newton Way. SN2 41 H3
Nightingale Rd. SN3 43 H3
Nightwood Copse. SN5 43 E5
Nindum Rd. SN3 46 D4
Norcliffe Rd. SN3 46 D4
Norfolk Clo. SN3 46 D2
Norman Rd. SN1 41 H6
North St. SN1 46 A3
North Star Av. SN2 45 G1
Northampton St. SN1 46 B2
Northbrook Rd. SN2 41 G5
Northern Rd. SN2 41 G6
Northfield Way. SN3 47 E1
Northleaze Clo. SN3 41 F4
Norton Gro. SN3 46 B2
Norwood Clo. SN3 47 F4
Noyes Clo. SN2 40 C2
Nuffield Clo. SN5 44 C1
Nuthatch Clo. SN3 47 G2
Nutmeg Clo. SN2 40 D3
Nyland Rd. SN3 47 E1
Nythe Rd. SN3 43 E5

Oak Garden. SN3 42 D3
Oak Tree Av. SN2 42 A4
Oakford Walk. SN3 46 D2
Oakham Clo. SN3 44 C3
Oakie Clo. SN3 41 G1
Oaksey Rd. SN2 41 H2
Oakwood Rd. SN5 44 C1
Oasthouse Clo. SN5 40 A6
Oberon Way. SN2 41 F2
Ocotol Way. SN1 46 B1
Odstock Rd. SN2 41 H1
Okebourne Pk. SN3 47 F5
Okeford Clo. SN3 47 E1
Okus Gro. SN2 42 B3
Okus Rd. SN1 45 F4
Old Mill La. SN3 46 B4
Old Shaw La. SN5 44 B1
Olive Gro. SN2 41 G4
Oliver Clo. SN5 44 A2
Omdurman St. SN2 41 H6
Orchard Gro. SN2 42 B3
Orchid Clo. SN3 41 H3
Oriel St. SN1 45 H2
Orkney Clo. SN5 44 B2
Orlando Clo. SN5 44 A3
Orrin Clo. SN5 40 C5
Orwell Clo. SN2 41 F2
Osborne St. SN2 41 G6
Osprey Clo. SN3 47 G2

Osterley Rd. SN2 41 E
Overbrooke. SN3 47 F
Overton Gdns. SN3 43 E
Owl Clo. SN3 47 G
Oxford Rd. SN3 42 D
Oxford St. SN1 45 G
Packington Clo. SN5 44 B
Paddington Dri. SN5 45 E
Paddock Clo. SN2 41 E
Pakenham Rd. SN3 47 E
Parham Walk. SN5 44 A
Park La. SN1 45 F
Park Side. SN3 42 D
Park Springs. SN5 44 D
Parklands Rd. SN3 46 E
Parr Clo. SN5 44 A
Parsley Clo. SN2 40 D
Parsonage Rd. SN3 42 D
Partridge Clo. SN3 47 H
Passmore Clo. SN3 47 G
Pasture Clo. SN2 45 E
Patney Walk. SN2 41 G
Paulet Clo. SN5 44 A
Peaks Down. SN5 40 B
Pearce Clo. SN2 42 C
Pearl Rd. SN5 44 A
Peatmoor Way. SN5 40 B
Pembroke Gdns. SN2 41 E
Pembroke St. SN1 45 G
Pen Clo. SN2 41 C
Pencarrow. SN2 41
Pendennis Rd. SN5 44 E
Penfold Gdns. SN1 45 H
Penhill Dri. SN2 41 H
Penny La. SN3 46 C
Pennycress Clo. SN2 41 E
Pentridge Clo. SN3 47
Penzance Dri. SN5 45 E
Pepperbox Hill. SN5 40 E
Percheron Clo. SN5 44 E
Percy St. SN2 45
Peregrine Clo. SN3 43
Periwinkle Clo. SN2 40 E
Petersfield Rd. SN3 47 E
Pevensey Way. SN5 44 E
Pewsham Rd. SN2 42 A
Pheasant Clo. SN3 47 C
Pickwick Clo. SN2 42 E
Picton Rd. SN5 44 E
Pigeon House La. SN3 42 E
Pilgrim Clo. SN5 44 E
Pilton Clo. SN5 40 A
Pinehurst Rd. SN2 41 C
Pinetree Rise. SN2 41 C
Pinnegar Way. SN3 47 C
Pinnocks Pl. SN2 42
Pioneer Clo. SN5 44 A
Pipers Way. SN3 46
Pipitdene. SN3 47
Plattes Clo. SN5 40
Pleydell Rd. SN1 46
Plymouth St. SN1 46
Poltondale. SN3 47
Pond St. SN2 41
Ponting St. SN2 46
Poole Rd. SN2 41
Pope Clo. SN2 41
Poplar Av. SN2 41
Popplechurch Dri. SN3 47
Portal Rd. SN2 41
Portland Av. SN1 45
Portmore Clo. SN5 40
Portsmouth St. SN1 46
Potterdown Rd. SN2 41
Poulton St. SN2
Pound La. SN2
Poynings Way. SN5 44
Primrose Clo. SN2 40
Princes St. SN1 46
Priory Rd. SN3 46
Pritchard Clo. SN2 42
Prospect Hill. SN1 46
Prospect Pl. SN1 46
Purbeck Clo. SN3 47
Purley Clo. SN3 47
Purley Rd. SN4 47
Purslane Clo. SN2 40
Purton Rd. SN2 40

Quarry Brook Clo. SN3 43
Quarry Mews. SN1 45
Quarry Rd. SN1 45
Queen Elizabeth Dri. SN2 40

69

WILTON

INDUSTRIAL & RETAIL:

WOOTTON BASSETT

INDUSTRIAL & RETAIL:

WROUGHTON

PLEASE NOTE: All maps, plans and indexes contained in this publication are strictly copyright. They may not be copied or reproduced in any way without prior permission of both Estate Publications and the Ordnance Survey.

Postcodes have been reproduced with permission of the Post Office. Every care has been taken by Estate Publications but the Post Office cannot be held responsible for any errors or omissions. The outward part of the Postcode which is reproduced in this index will not suffice in identifying a particular address. The list of Postcodes is a copyright work of the Post Office. Edition 184 H 7.00

ESTATE PUBLICATIONS

LOCAL RED BOOKS

ALDERSHOT, CAMBERLEY
ALFRETON, BELPER, RIPLEY
ASHFORD, TENTERDEN
BANGOR, CAERNARFON
BARNSTAPLE, ILFRACOMBE
BASILDON, BILLERICAY
BASINGSTOKE, ANDOVER
BATH, BRADFORD-ON-AVON
BEDFORD
BOURNEMOUTH, POOLE, CHRISTCHURCH
BRACKNELL
BRENTWOOD
BRIGHTON, LEWES, NEWHAVEN, SEAFORD
BRISTOL
BROMLEY (London Bromley)
BURTON-UPON-TRENT, SWADLINCOTE
BURY ST. EDMUNDS
CAMBRIDGE
CARDIFF
CARLISLE
CHELMSFORD, BRAINTREE, MALDON, WITHAM
CHESTER
CHESTERFIELD
CHICHESTER, BOGNOR REGIS
COATBRIDGE, AIRDRIE
COLCHESTER, CLACTON
CORBY, KETTERING
CRAWLEY & MID SUSSEX
CREWE
DERBY, HEANOR, CASTLE DONINGTON
EASTBOURNE, BEXHILL, SEAFORD, NEWHAVEN
EDINBURGH, MUSSELBURGH, PENICUIK
EXETER, EXMOUTH
FAREHAM, GOSPORT
FALKIRK, GRANGEMOUTH
FLINTSHIRE TOWNS
FOLKESTONE, DOVER, DEAL & ROMNEY MARSH
GLASGOW, & PAISLEY
GLOUCESTER, CHELTENHAM
GRAVESEND, DARTFORD
GRAYS, THURROCK
GREAT YARMOUTH, LOWESTOFT
GRIMSBY, CLEETHORPES
GUILDFORD, WOKING
HAMILTON, MOTHERWELL, EAST KILBRIDE
HARLOW, BISHOPS STORTFORD
HASTINGS, BEXHILL, RYE
HEREFORD
HERTFORD, HODDESDON, WARE
HIGH WYCOMBE
HUNTINGDON, ST. NEOTS
IPSWICH, FELIXSTOWE
ISLE OF WIGHT TOWNS
KENDAL
KIDDERMINSTER
KINGSTON-UPON-HULL
LANCASTER, MORECAMBE
LEICESTER, LOUGHBOROUGH
LINCOLN
LLANDUDNO, COLWYN BAY
LUTON, DUNSTABLE
MACCLESFIELD
MAIDSTONE
MANSFIELD, MANSFIELD WOODHOUSE
MEDWAY, GILLINGHAM
MILTON KEYNES
NEW FOREST TOWNS
NEWPORT, CHEPSTOW
NEWTOWN, WELSHPOOL
NORTHAMPTON
NORTHWICH, WINSFORD
NORWICH
NOTTINGHAM, EASTWOOD, HUCKNALL, ILKESTON
OXFORD, ABINGDON
PENZANCE, ST. IVES
PETERBOROUGH
PLYMOUTH, IVYBRIDGE, SALTASH, TORPOINT
PORTSMOUTH, HAVANT, WATERLOOVILLE
READING
REDDITCH, BROMSGROVE
REIGATE, BANSTEAD, LEATHERHEAD, DORKING
RHYL, PRESTATYN
RUGBY

ST. ALBANS, WELWYN, HATFIELD
SALISBURY, AMESBURY, WILTON
SCUNTHORPE
SEVENOAKS
SHREWSBURY
SITTINGBOURNE, FAVERSHAM, ISLE OF SHEPPEY
SLOUGH, MAIDENHEAD, WINDSOR
SOUTHAMPTON, EASTLEIGH
SOUTHEND-ON-SEA
STAFFORD
STEVENAGE, HITCHIN, LETCHWORTH
STIRLING
STOKE-ON-TRENT
STROUD, NAILSWORTH
SWANSEA, NEATH, PORT TALBOT
SWINDON, CHIPPENHAM, MARLBOROUGH
TAUNTON, BRIDGWATER
TELFORD
THANET, CANTERBURY, HERNE BAY, WHITSTABLE
TORBAY (Torquay, Paignton, Newton Abbot)
TRURO, FALMOUTH
TUNBRIDGE WELLS, TONBRIDGE, CROWBOROUGH
WARWICK, ROYAL LEAMINGTON SPA &
    STRATFORD UPON AVON
WATFORD, HEMEL HEMPSTEAD
WELLINGBOROUGH
WESTON-SUPER-MARE, CLEVEDON
WEYMOUTH, DORCHESTER
WINCHESTER, NEW ARLESFORD
WORCESTER, DROITWICH
WORTHING, LITTLEHAMPTON, ARUNDEL
WREXHAM
YORK

COUNTY RED BOOKS (Town Centre Maps)

BEDFORDSHIRE
BERKSHIRE
BUCKINGHAMSHIRE
CAMBRIDGESHIRE
CHESHIRE
CORNWALL
DERBYSHIRE
DEVON
DORSET
ESSEX
GLOUCESTERSHIRE
HAMPSHIRE
HEREFORDSHIRE
HERTFORDSHIRE
KENT
LEICESTERSHIRE & RUTLAND
LINCOLNSHIRE
NORFOLK
NORTHAMPTONSHIRE
NOTTINGHAMSHIRE
OXFORDSHIRE
SHROPSHIRE
SOMERSET
STAFFORDSHIRE
SUFFOLK
SURREY
SUSSEX (EAST)
SUSSEX (WEST)
WILTSHIRE
WORCESTERSHIRE

OTHER MAPS

KENT TO CORNWALL (1:460,000)
COUNTY MAP - DORSET
            - SOMERSET
            - WILTSHIRE
CHINA (1:6,000,000)
INDIA (1:3,750,000)
INDONESIA (1:4,000,000)
NEPAL (1,800,000)
SOUTH EAST ASIA (1:6,000,000)
THAILAND (1:1,600,000)

STREET PLANS

EDINBURGH TOURIST PLAN
ST. ALBANS

OFFICIAL TOURIST & LEISURE MAPS

SOUTH EAST ENGLAND (1:200,000)
KENT & EAST SUSSEX (1:150,000)
SUSSEX & SURREY (1:150,000)
SUSSEX (1:50,000)
SOUTHERN ENGLAND (1:200,000)
ISLE OF WIGHT (1:50,000)
WESSEX (1:200,000)
DORSET (1:50,000)
DEVON & CORNWALL (1:200,000)
CORNWALL (1:180,000)
DEVON (1:200,000)
DARTMOOR & SOUTH DEVON COAST (1:100,000)
EXMOOR & NORTH DEVON COAST (1:100,000)
GREATER LONDON M25 (1:80,000)
EAST ANGLIA (1:200,000)
CHILTERNS & THAMES VALLEY (1:200,000)
THE COTSWOLDS (1:110,000)
COTSWOLDS & WYEDEAN (1:200,000)
WALES (1:250,000)
CYMRU (1:250,000)
THE SHIRES OF MIDDLE ENGLAND (1:250,000)
THE MID SHIRES (Staffs, Shrops, etc.) (1:200,000)
PEAK DISTRICT (1:100,000)
SNOWDONIA (1:125,000)
YORKSHIRE (1:200,000)
YORKSHIRE DALES (1:125,000)
NORTH YORKSHIRE MOORS (1:125,000)
NORTH WEST ENGLAND (1:200,000)
ISLE OF MAN (1:60,000)
NORTH PENNINES & LAKES (1:200,000)
LAKE DISTRICT (1:75,000)
BORDERS OF ENGLAND & SCOTLAND (1:200,000)
BURNS COUNTRY (1:200,000)
HEART OF SCOTLAND (1:200,000)
GREATER GLASGOW (1:150,000)
EDINBURGH & THE LOTHIANS (1:150,000)
ISLE OF ARRAN (1:63,360)
FIFE (1:100,000)
LOCH LOMOND & TROSSACHS (1:150,000)
ARGYLL THE ISLES & LOCH LOMOND (1:275,000)
PERTHSHIRE, DUNDEE & ANGUS (1:150,000)
FORT WILLIAM, BEN NEVIS, GLEN COE (1:185,000)
IONA (1:10,000) & MULL (1:115,000)
GRAMPIAN HIGHLANDS (1:185,000)
LOCH NESS & INVERNESS (1:150,000)
AVIEMORE & SPEY VALLEY (1:150,000)
SKYE & LOCHALSH (1:130,000)
ARGYLL & THE ISLES (1:200,000)
CAITHNESS & SUTHERLAND (1:185,000)
HIGHLANDS OF SCOTLAND (1:275,000)
WESTERN ISLES (1:125,000)
ORKNEY & SHETLAND (1:128,000)
ENGLAND & WALES (1:650,000)
SCOTLAND (1:500,000)
HISTORIC SCOTLAND (1:500,000)
SCOTLAND CLAN MAP (1:1,625,000)
BRITISH ISLES (1:1,100,000)
GREAT BRITAIN (1:1,100,000)

EUROPEAN LEISURE MAPS

EUROPE (1:3,100,000)
BENELUX (1:600,000)
FRANCE (1:1,000,000)
GERMANY (1:1,000,000)
IRELAND (1:625,000)
ITALY (1:1,000,000)
SPAIN & PORTUGAL (1,1,000,000)
CROSS CHANNEL VISITORS' MAP (1:530,000)
WORLD (1:35,000,000)
WORLD FLAT

TOWNS IN NORTHERN FRANCE STREET ATLAS
BOULOGNE SHOPPERS MAP
CALAIS SHOPPERS MAP
DIEPPE SHOPPERS MAP

ESTATE PUBLICATIONS are also
Distributors in the UK for:

INTERNATIONAL TRAVEL MAPS, Canada
HALLWAG, Switzerland
ORDNANCE SURVEY

Catalogue and prices from:
ESTATE PUBLICATIONS
Bridewell House, Tenterden, Kent. TN30 6EP.
Tel: 01580 764225   Fax: 01580 763720
www.estate-publications.co.uk